I'VE SEEN
HEAVEN

Sarah Gardner

•••

ISBN: 979-8-218-17493-4

CONTENTS

INTRODUCTION
Pastor Sarah Gardner

I could start this book by telling you of my business successes. Many people have asked me how I built a multi-million-dollar apartment business. When I came from Italy to America, I was dirt poor. I became a millionaire, and now my children and grandchildren are millionaires.

God supernaturally gave me the ability to obtain wealth through my business. Just as an example, when the 2008 recession hit in the U.S., I had bought a 9-million-dollar property. God led me to a person who advised me on how to talk to the bank to adjust my mortgage due to the recession. The bank adjusted my mortgage, reducing the balance by 5 million dollars. In just one transaction, God made me 5 million dollars. I felt like Isaac, who during a time of famine, was prospered by God. I could tell you of many more transactions.

Because God has always provided abundantly, I was able to pour my time and treasure into God's work. I founded six churches and mentored many disciples. I never received any money from the ministry, and I never will. So, why did I write this book? I didn't write this book to make money, because every penny will go back into ministry. And it's not to make a name for myself. This book is to tell my story for God's glory. You see, God rescued my life from destruction. I have experienced the supernatural life and seen first-hand what eternity holds. I am forever grateful that God made Himself real to me.

I hope that this book helps you pursue Him diligently. The more you pursue Him, the more He will reveal Himself to you. I am a great believer that what God does for one, He will do for another because He is no respecter of persons (Acts 10:34).

People describe me as petite of stature but big at heart. My husband says, *"Sarah is feisty, full of life and comes alive when she tells people about her God. She is highly entrepreneurial, self-motivated, and one who tells it straight; she does not beat around the bush."* Even in reading this book, you will see that I don't use a lot of fancy words. I learned English as a second language later in life, but I speak about my experiences from my heart. I studied Jesus and picked up His ways to always be truthful. I want my life to always reflect Him.

Now that you know a little about me, let's go on this journey together.

CHAPTER ONE
The Early Years

I was born in a little town in Italy called San Chirico Nuovo, a Province of Potenza, Basilicata. My parents named me Margherita Maggio, but everyone in Italy called me Marietta. When I came to America, everyone just called me Marie, for simplicity's sake. After I was born again, God changed my name to Sarah; I will talk about this later.

When I was born, my mother was 43 years old, and my father was 53. My parents already had 5 children. They did not expect or want another child this late in their lives. They were at the peak of their success with their farming business, and they were very busy. A baby was an interference they could not accept.

My mother would have aborted me if abortions had been safe in those days. Instead, my parents decided to stop feeding me. My sister, Philomena, who was ten years old when I was born, would take me to mothers in our neighborhood who were nursing their own babies, and say, *"My mother is not home. Please, can you feed my sister?"* In my small village, everyone knew each other so it was not unusual to do this. My parents did not know why I was still living.

Eventually, I was not fed enough and I became very weak.

One day, Mr. Zasa, a painter, who was also our next-door neighbor, was painting inside our house thinking no one was home. He heard heavy breathing and went to see where the breathing was coming from. When he saw this baby in the bed gasping for breath, he stopped painting and immediately took me to the doctor. Whatever the doctor did that day, I do not know, but afterward, Mr. Zasa started feeding me soft food and I started recovering. Mr. Zasa and his wife, Rosa, told my mother, *"If you do not want this baby, we will take her."* That is when my parents realized that the Zasas had caught on to their plan to let me starve. After that, my mother started taking care of me.

The Zasas saved my life. Even though they were poor and had five children, they were Christians and would have made the sacrifice to raise me. They kept this situation to themselves. Their family moved to northern Italy when I was twenty, and we lost contact. When I was forty-one years old, I went back to visit Italy, and I stopped by to see them. I wanted to tell them that I had become a Christian like them. That is when the Zasas felt the freedom to tell me what really happened, and that God had used them to save my life.

•••

When I was ten years old, my mother became ill and for ten years, I took care of her. She was bedridden much of the time. My mother went from hospital to hospital. Whichever hospital my mother was taken to, I went with her because in those days, there were not enough nurses to take care of the sick and their families were required to help. The hospitals were quite far away from our village, so I stayed with her the whole time.

The reason I was the only one taking care of my mother was because my siblings were much older than I was. All of them were already married and raising their children. My father was managing our three farms, so I became my mother's caretaker. I became very close to her during her illness, however, from the time I was 10 to 20 years old, I missed out on a good part of my childhood and education.

When I was twenty, my mother died. I was devasted because she was my friend and my everything. My father was beside himself. He and I never had much of a relationship. As a child, I was afraid of him. He often became angry and had sharp arguments with my oldest brother and my mother. Now, there was only my father and me. The devastation over my mother's death made the tension of living with my father very difficult.

•••

About two years after my mother's death, I was out on the porch one day when a handsome man passed by. I caught his eye, and he caught mine. His name was Mike. I did not know who he was, but I found out that Mike was originally from my hometown. He was twelve years older than I was and had moved to America twelve years earlier. He inquired about me, and we started seeing each other.

At twenty-two years of age, I was married and within two months moved across the ocean to Detroit, Michigan in America. I became pregnant on my honeymoon and had my first son (Anthony) during my first year in America. My second son (Dino) was born the following year, and my daughter (Tracy) was born sixteen months later. Within four years, I had three children.

We moved from Detroit to the city of Warren. One day from my porch, I heard some people talking in Italian. I realized that our new neighbors were Italian. I was so happy to hear Italian that I went over to introduce myself. Her name was Maria Carlissimo, and she was thirty years older than I was. We connected right away and over the next few months we became very close friends. Maria loved my children like a grandmother. As our relationship grew, Maria became like a mother to me, and she felt like I was her daughter.

Maria had her son's car but didn't know how to drive it. I didn't have a car, but I knew how to drive and began to take Maria to the doctor, the store, and all the personal errands she needed. Maria and her son managed a forty-unit apartment complex in Windsor, Ontario, which was about one hour away from my home. Her son knew how to speak English, but he had started another business and he did not have time to manage the apartment complex anymore. He suggested that I drive Maria to the apartment complex and become her interpreter.

Before long, Maria asked me to manage the complex myself. This is where I learned how to manage apartments. This was a blessing God had prepared for me without me even knowing it. Maria was so pleased with how well I was managing her business that she wanted to buy another complex closer to where we lived in the United States. She would put up the money, and I would manage it. We would become partners. When I told my husband Mike, he said, *"No, I am Mormon, and Maria is Catholic. You cannot go into business with her."* He stopped me from working with Maria after that.

At this point, I felt that I had already learned so much about managing apartments, I thought, *"why should I let all this knowledge of how to do this business go to waste?"* I started looking into doing this business for myself, but I did not have enough money for a down payment. I knew a couple in the Mormon church named Pat and Frank Lombardi. In conversation, Pat had told me that they had $12,000 in the bank. I found a rundown complex that could be purchased for $5,000 down. I asked the Lombardi's to lend me $5,000, and I said I would give them double what the bank was giving them in interest. They agreed and loaned it to me. So, I bought my first apartment complex of 12 rundown units.

After six months, the business had earned the $5,000 to return to the Lombardis but they said, *"If you need it, as long as you pay us this kind of interest, go ahead and keep it."* So, I took that $5,000 and bought another rundown eleven-unit complex. Two years later, I sold those two complexes and bought a less rundown 120-unit complex in a much better area. But there were 35 apartments that were vacant, and I had to work very hard to fill them.

•••

The business grew. In seven years, I had 435 apartment units. I credit God who was guiding me, and Maria Carlissimo, who introduced me to the business. By the time I was thirty-eight I owned a thriving apartment business. I lived in a 7,000 square-foot dream-home that could have been featured in a magazine. All the furniture was imported from France and Italy. I owned two Cadillacs. My kids could go to any college they wanted because we had the money. From the outside, it appeared I had everything but, on the inside, I was dying. I was so depressed. The depression took over and I became fearful in my own home.

The only place I felt safe was in a tiny spot beside the kitchen sink. I built a small bed there and huddled in it. I slept there for months and would dream that I was happier dead than alive. I called one of my friends from the Mormon church, Barbara Mangiapane, and told her, *"I think I want to join my relatives in Heaven. When I think about death it gives me peace."*

CHAPTER TWO

My Troubled Marriage

For eighteen years, my husband Mike worked during the day at a General Motors car plant and volunteered most evenings at the Mormon church. Because of that, I was always alone. I felt like he had two jobs. Early on in our marriage, I couldn't make friends because I did not know how to speak English, but I gradually learned English by attending the Mormon church.

Mike was a deacon in the Mormon church, so he had many responsibilities. On Sundays, he was at the church from 7:00 a.m. until 8:00 p.m. Monday nights after work, he went to visit the sick. On Tuesday nights, he had a meeting with all the leaders. Wednesday nights, he had regular church service and Thursday nights, he was at a study of the book of Mormon. On Saturdays, we went to clean the church and shop for groceries. I wanted Mike to stay home more often. I needed him at home, but he was too busy with the church. I could not convince him that both his wife and children needed his time and attention. I felt like I was a single parent for many years.

To make matters worse, Mike would go every other week on

mission trips to Grand River in Canada. When I tried to complain about him being gone so much, Mike would say, *"You are just a little girl, and you don't know anything; grow up!"* Because he was older than I was and a deacon in the Mormon church, I thought I was the one in the wrong. I would reason with myself, *"After all, he is not going to bars or having affairs with other women."* Yet, I couldn't shake the loneliness. We were strangers co-habiting in the same house, and we rarely spoke to each other. He was not available for me or our three children. So, I tried to be both a mother and father. My children saw how Mike and I struggled in our marriage, and they took advantage of that. As time went on, they became more disobedient and rebellious.

•••

As my kids became teenagers, they grew more independent. I felt like they did not need me anymore. The wealth we had accumulated didn't take away my loneliness. I was totally empty inside. I concluded that Mike did not want to be with me. My kids made me feel like they didn't need me either. My three brothers, two sisters, and their families were all in Italy. I had reached a point of desperation. One thing I needed was for my husband to be my friend. I wanted to talk to him and share my thoughts with him, but he didn't have the same needs. I felt rejected. My children often found me crying because I was in such great pain.

I felt like I was dying. From the first Saturday night I arrived in America, I suffered from painful headaches every day. My head throbbed so hard I screamed in pain. I would wrap a scarf around my head because I felt like my head was going to pop open. It was the only way I found a little relief. I went to a doctor who prescribed medication, and I improved somewhat. After a few months, however, the headaches returned. My body became immune to the medication and the pain returned. One doctor who treated me several times finally said, "*We don't know what else to do with this headache.*"

My vision had declined to the point that four feet away, I could only see shadows. I didn't know if I was going blind or what and this really weighed on me. I do not know if this was because I had been crying every single day since I came to America. I used to blame God and say, "*Why did you bring me to this country to make me suffer like this?*"

Many days I had pain in my knees that almost immobilized me. The only time I felt relief is when I wrapped wool around my knees. I felt that there was no end to my miserable life. I didn't believe in divorce. None of my siblings or extended family in Italy were divorced. In the Mormon church, there were two women who were divorced. They were looked upon like they had a plague. Those divorced women were not allowed to receive communion. They were shunned by the leaders and the people.

My marriage was deeply troubled, but I could not portray that to others. I had to portray the image of a dedicated wife. I was living two lives, one way at the church and another at home, and it was exhausting. Since I was sick and divorce was not an option, I thought there was no way out.

CHAPTER THREE

Suicide or Salvation

On a cold and snowy winter day in Michigan, my husband was not home, and my children were in school. I was alone, and life seemed hopeless. Out of my desperation, at thirty-eight years of age, I had come to the end of myself and decided to end my life. I walked over to the bathroom medicine cabinet and pulled out a bottle of tranquilizers. I thought to myself, *"Take all of them. These pills will end the pain. No one will miss me."*

I walked into my family room, with the pills in my right hand and a glass of water in my left hand. For some strange reason, I decided to turn on the television for background noise. As I was walking toward the kitchen to take the pills, I heard a man say, *"I see a little mama…you're going to kill yourself."* I turned around and saw the man on television, who had his eyes closed. I thought, *"how does he know what I am about to do?"*

The man continued, *"You don't need to do that. You think you want to end your life today, but if you do what I'm going to tell you to do, your life will change for the better and God will be with you helping you live. Just invite Jesus to come into your heart and today you will start living."*

He continued, *"You have been a good person all your life. You've done mission work. You've been water baptized. You've done many good things for people. You've faithfully attended church, but you've never received Jesus into your heart."*

I had never heard that before. I thought, *"how do I receive Jesus into my heart? Should I just crack open my chest and let Him in?"* I stared at the television in total shock. How in the world does this man know me? Even though I didn't understand everything I was hearing, I knew he was speaking to me, and I kept listening. This man continued, *"You can stand up or kneel down. Do whatever is most comfortable for you. As a matter of fact, if you say this prayer after me, you will begin to live today. Just repeat these words after me."*

At that moment I thought, *"what do I have to lose?"* I knelt down in front of the television and repeated the words after him. While I was speaking those words, I felt like a bucket of warm water was being poured on top of my head and flowing down my body. As I looked up at the television, I saw the man clearly. I thought, *"Oh my, a miracle has happened, I got my eyesight back."* The migraine headache instantly vanished, and the pain in my knees stopped. I thought, *"what's happening to me?"* I was in awe.

For the first time, I knew God had touched me and He became real to me. I felt accepted and loved like no one had ever loved me before. All my life, I experienced rejection and abandonment. Now something new was happening to me. I was overtaken by love and acceptance. At the end of the prayer, the man who was speaking to me from the television said, *"If you've prayed this prayer for the first time, you need to call someone to affirm what you've done. Start reading the Bible every day. Even two or three chapters a day. But make sure you read it every day."* I later learned that this man was Pat Robertson of the 700 Club.

When my kids came home from school that day, they noticed an immediate difference. I didn't tell them right away what had happened, except they could tell that I could see clearly, and I didn't have a headache. They later told me that they thought maybe I was on some new drug. As they saw the changes in me - from depressed to joyful and loving, they became more curious. They saw me becoming more patient and more peaceful. They liked it but thought that this was a new fad that was going to wear out.

CHAPTER FOUR

By His Stripes I Am Healed

I remained in awe for days and I wanted to do everything Pat Robertson told me to do. I started looking for a Bible in the house, but I only found books pertaining to Mormonism. One week later, I was making my son Anton's bed and noticed a little pocket Bible on his nightstand. Someone had given it to him, but this Bible had never been opened. The print was so small, but my eyes were now clear and I could read it without a problem.

That day, and for the next eight weeks, I read up to seven hours a day. I thought, *"this is the best kept secret ever! Why didn't anyone ever tell me about this?"* Several times Mike had walked into the family room while I was reading my Bible. More than once he said, *"Stay away from that book! That Bible will make you lose your mind!"* I knew my mind was changing for the better, because the thoughts of depression and the things that were bothering me before, were not bothering me anymore.

I kept reading the Bible and receiving more revelation. The situation with Mike had not changed, he still was neglecting me, and he still was rarely home. Actually – things got worse because he did not want me to read the Bible. Those things did not bother me like before, because I was in my own new world with God, who loved me and accepted me.

About four months later, Mike saw me reading and asked me, "By the way, who taught you how to read English?" When he said that, I became aware that I had been reading English. I thought, *"Wow! God did another miracle for me."* God taught me to read English and comprehend what I was reading.

Since the day I received Jesus in my heart, I had become a new person. I frequently remember something else Pat Robertson said on the 700 Club: *"Instead of dying today, you will start living."* That's what happened the day I received Jesus into my heart; I started living. And the more I read the Bible, the healthier, stronger, and younger I felt.

I suffered for so long because I was lacking knowledge of the Bible. The Bible says, *"My people are destroyed for lack of knowledge..."* (Hosea 4:6). I was one who was being destroyed. But, the more I read the Bible, the more I understood what Jesus did for me.

I came across Isaiah 53, and I realized that Jesus had done the great exchange for me. He became sick, so I could be healed. He became poor, so I could be well supplied. He took my sorrow so I could have joy. Jesus had already done everything for me through the finished work of the cross.

I began to discover truth after truth:

Jesus was punished so I can be forgiven.
Jesus was wounded so I can be healed. (1 Peter 2:24)
Jesus was made one with my sinfulness, so I can be righteous with His righteousness. (2 Corinthians 5:21)

Jesus died my death so I can share His life.

Jesus was made a curse for me so I can receive His blessings.

Jesus became poor with my poverty so I can enjoy His wealth. (2 Corinthians 8:9)

Jesus bore my shame so I can share His glory.

Jesus endured my rejection so I can be accepted. (Ephesians 1:23)

My old nature was crucified with Jesus so my new nature could come to life.

One Saturday, I was feeling so strong that I started cleaning the house. I got carried away and overdid it. I hurt my back badly. Because I had already read Isaiah 53:5, *"And by His stripes we are healed"*, I said repeatedly, *"Jesus took my pain. I don't have to have this pain. By Jesus' stripes, I am healed."* Early Sunday morning, something cracked in my back and the pain went away. I was totally healed. I couldn't wait to go to the Mormon church for the Sunday afternoon testimony service and tell everybody what had happened to me.

CHAPTER FIVE

Testifying to the Mormon Church

Sunday mornings at the Mormon church was their traditional service, but in the afternoon, they had what they called a testimony service. I attended those services for nearly twenty years but had never testified. Mike used to get upset with me for not testifying. He would say, *"You never testify. You need to testify. You make me look bad."* I would say to Mike, *"I have nothing to testify about."*

Because Mike had become a minister by this time, it would have made him look good for me to testify. But up until this point, I did not have anything good to testify about. I had been unhappy our whole marriage because he was one way at the church, but at home he was neglecting me. In all good conscience, I could not testify. So, I never did.

But when my back was healed, no one had to tell me to testify because I had something to testify about, and I wanted to give God the glory. I also wanted to let the Mormon people, who I loved, know that they could be healed too by the Word of God.

When the testimony service started, there were no more than 75-80 people. I was the first one to get up, and I told the people that I had been healed. I told them about the Word, which says, *"by Jesus' stripes, I am healed,"* I said, *"Look at me, I'm fine."* After I said that, it was so quiet, you could have heard a pin drop. As I looked around, I could read the body language that no one got what I said. I could tell that Mike was embarrassed. It was an awkward moment.

No one said anything to me afterward except one couple, Spencer Evert and his wife, who came up to me and pulled me aside. Spencer's wife smiled and we spoke.

Mrs. Evert: *"You are one of us."*

Me: *"What do you mean, one of you?"*

Mrs. Evert: *"We are born again like you. We noticed how you testified. That is how we knew you were born again."*

Me: *"How did it happen to you?"*

Mr. and Mrs. Evert: *"Through Fred Price, an evangelist on TV."*

Me: *"Oh, I understand, I was born-again through Pat Robertson of the 700 Club."*

Ms. Evert put her index finger in front of her mouth. *"Shh. The people here they are like the Pharisees. They don't understand what we are talking about."* She then told me, *"We go to the Full Gospel Businessmen's Fellowship meetings once a month. If you want to go, we will pick you up and we will take you with us."*

Me: *"Yes, yes, I would like to go."*

Mrs. Evert: *"But you are going to promise me not to tell anyone from this church. They won't understand."*

Me: *"I promise, I won't say a word."*

But as I said those words, I was bothered because I thought, *"If this gospel is the best kept secret, why should I keep it to myself?"*

CHAPTER SIX

The Authority of The Believer

When I went to the Full Gospel Businessmen's meeting with Spencer Evert and his wife, there was a table with hundreds of books on it. My eyes went right to a book, *The Believer's Authority* by Kenneth E. Hagin. I bought it, started reading, and could not put it down. That book taught me that God had put Adam in charge of the earth and gave him authority and dominion over the earth. When the devil deceived Adam, the devil took the authority and dominion that God had given him. When Jesus came to earth, He took back the authority and dominion the devil stole from Adam. When we receive Jesus as our Lord and Savior, Jesus gives to us the same authority and dominion.

Now, because we have this authority and dominion, we as Christians need to live our lives from a "new creation" point of view. 2 Corinthians 5:17 says, *"Therefore, if anyone is in Christ, he is a new creation; old things have passed away; behold, all things have become new."* When I understood these things as presented through scripture in *The Believers Authority*, I thought, *"Oh, wow! Where have I been? This is the best kept secret ever - people do not know and they need to know.*" I understood that God needs us to reach unbelievers and that we are the "little Jesus'" with skin on. We are God's representatives on earth. This is why we as believers, live from a "new creation" point of view.

A burning desire came upon me to tell others about what I had learned from the book - *The Believer's Authority.* I thought, *"how do I do that?"* I had read how the Apostle Paul reached people where they were at. In 1 Corinthians 9:19-20 it says, *"For though I am free from all men, I have made myself a servant to all, that I might win the more; and to the Jews I became as a Jew, that I might win Jews; to those who are under the law, as under the law, that I might win those who are under the law..."*(NKJV)

Many people I knew that weren't Mormon, were Catholic, and I wanted to reach them with the things I was learning. I thought, *"if I teach a Bible study in a Catholic Church, the Catholic people will feel comfortable attending it there."* I asked a few people if they would like to do a Bible study at the Catholic Church to learn more about Jesus. When I had a few people agree to come, I went to the priest at the Catholic Church near me. Because I am Italian, he assumed I was Catholic. I asked the priest if he would give us a room for a Bible study, and he said yes. So I started meeting with the people at the Catholic Church. I prepared the lessons based on *The Believer's Authority* book.

I had never been trained in doing this, but I took a leap of faith. My native language was Italian for both reading and writing, but this was an English-speaking group. I used to be insecure about speaking English because I struggled to put full sentences together, but I wanted the people to learn about this book, and that driving force made me overcome my insecurity. The people would help me pronounce words I did not say right, and we often laughed together as they helped me do so. To my surprise, the people did not mind and really enjoyed helping me. I would have someone read the scripture verses, then I would explain the verses. So even though we had a language barrier, they liked what they were learning. Before long, that Bible study grew to 40 people.

One night during the Bible study, the priest of that Catholic Church came by, and he saw that the group had grown and he was really pleased. After we were done with the meeting that night, the priest asked me, *"Next week, can I teach your Bible study?"* I said, *"Well, of course, this is your church."*

So, the priest came to the Bible study to teach the people. The priest did well - he taught us how Jesus did so many wonderful things while He was on Earth and then he talked about all the wonderful things that Jesus is going to do when he comes back.

I asked a question. I said, *"Father, Jesus came and did all these wonderful things and he's going to do wonderful things when he comes back. What about us in between, what do we do now?"* The priest thought that I was being sarcastic by asking that question, but I was sincere. After he heard my question, he got upset with me and said, *"You should not ask questions like that!"* Before I could say a word, the women and a couple of the men spoke up and said, *"Wait a minute, this is not a bad question. We also want to know what we are to do in between."* My question caused quite a stir.

I could tell the priest was upset – he glared at me saying, *"I want to see you in my office after this meeting."* The people were all dumbfounded by priest's reaction. After the meeting, I went into his office and the priest said, *"You are dismissed from this Bible study."*

Since I had the phone numbers of all the people I taught and they had mine, we reconnected. Most of them came to my house and we continued our weekly Bible study in my home. The Bible study did not stop with my dismissal from the church. It caused us to press in more.

I had learned that the power of God is in me, and the ability of God is in me. The authority that was in Jesus, God put it in me! I was so excited and those coming to the Bible study had the same reaction. They became so excited about learning these truths! Because I had never heard these things taught before, I was even more motivated to get the Word of God out to as many as I could reach.

What was different between my Bible study and other Bible studies? Those who came were eager to develop what they had received - that was the difference. It was not just about coming to hear a message, we learned that it was about putting the Word of God in action. I showed them who they are in Christ Jesus and how to activate that power in their lives.

The biblical truths explained in *The Believer's Authority* book were bringing so many answers to my life and to the lives of those who were attending the Bible study. That book had such a major impact on my life that this thought came to me repeatedly, *"I must find a church that teaches me like this book."* I prayed often that God would lead me to such a church.

I went to a large church of 2,000 people and after a while, the Lord told me, *"What they do here is good, but what I want you to learn, you are not going to learn here."* Then I went to another church that had 3,000 people. It was very popular, and the worship was good. But God told me the same thing, *"What they do here is good, but what I want you to learn, you are not going to learn here."* I tried church after church. Eventually, I stopped searching.

CHAPTER SEVEN

First Visit to Heaven

Two years after I received Jesus in my heart, I had gone to bed as usual. When I laid down, I prayed, *"God, all I know is that I was sick and now I am miraculously healed. Before, I was afraid to get close to people, but now I have a need to be with people. I had no love for humanity, but now I love everyone and yet, I want to know you even more."*

After I said this to God, I was pondering my thoughts lying there in the bed. Suddenly, there I was, standing by my bed, looking at another body just like mine. I thought, *"Oh my God, that's my body lying in bed."* My second body looked exactly like my physical body, and I was in amazement that I had two bodies. I noticed my husband lying next to me in bed. I called his name several times, but he didn't respond. It was as if he couldn't hear me. I wanted to wake him up to show him my two bodies. I wanted to tell him what was happening to me. I touched his shoulder and shook him, trying to wake him up, but he didn't wake up.

Then I went to my daughter's room to tell her, *"Come see; I have two bodies."* No matter how much I tried to wake her up, I couldn't.

I stared at her for a moment and then walked to my sons' rooms. I did the same thing to them, but they didn't respond either. I wanted to show them that I had two bodies and what was happening to me. I started floating off the ground and went downstairs to the kitchen, then floated down to the basement. One minute I was walking, and the next minute I was floating around the house. I thought to myself, *"this is fun!"* Then I returned to my bedroom, and again I was staring at my body that was in bed.

Suddenly, as I was staring at my body, I was sucked up like a vacuum. I found myself in Heaven. Jesus had been waiting for me. He was standing in front of me. There was a big bronze gate behind Him. He looked at me with welcoming eyes! Jesus said, *"I have been waiting for you."* His complexion was a deep tan, like he was from the Middle East, and His eyes communicated pure love. He was wearing a long white robe with a sash wrapped around His waist. He was about 5'11" tall. I thought, *"Jesus is the same height as my son, Anton."*

The energy coming from Jesus radiated love, kindness, and compassion. It penetrated my body and bones and into my heart. My whole being was filled with such light and warmth, and it surrounded me like a soft blanket. My body felt limitless. Jesus took me by the hand and said, *"Let me give you a tour and show you what we do here. I want to show you how we worship."* He led me onward and I followed. We walked through the bronze gate. I saw fields of different-colored tulips everywhere I looked. There was a constant aroma of flowers around me all the time. I felt love all around me coming from everything. Everything is alive in Heaven. Nothing can die.

As I was walking, I was reluctant to walk, because I thought I was going to crush the flowers. I stepped forward and crushed a flower and felt very bad about it. Jesus looked at me and said, *"Don't feel bad because nothing can be destroyed in Heaven."* I looked behind me and the flower I had stepped on was up and just as perfect as before. I understood that everything was created to worship God, even the trees and the flowers. The trees were worshiping God by their branches brushing together. I thought, *"this sounds like what I had read in Isaiah 55:12, that all the trees shall clap their hands."*

Jesus showed me different areas of Heaven. In one area, people lived simply in small spaces. They were sitting on the ground in little plots of 8 feet by 8 feet, with no roof over their heads. These people had come to believe in Jesus, but never did much on Earth for God or others. While they lived on Earth, they lived an honest and clean life, but they never told other people about God. They never expressed what they believed. Yet, they were happy because there is no sadness in Heaven.

I saw a woman I knew on Earth who was living in one of these small spaces, but she was happy. Jesus told me, *"She never did anything for me and my kingdom nor for the body of Christ while on Earth. Although she lived a clean life, she lived only for herself and for her family. She never did any good deeds for someone else."* I thought of the scripture that said, *"...Every man shall receive his own reward according to his own labour"* (1 Corinthians 3:8, KJV). Jesus explained this verse to me. *"When people on Earth receive me as their Savior, they make it to Heaven. If they do not live for me by loving their neighbors as their selves and tell others of their conversion, they do not receive any rewards."*

In another area of Heaven, I saw homes that were teepees. As Jesus and I walked, He explained that the people who lived in the teepees had told a few people about the Lord, helped a few people, and did some good deeds. After I came back from Heaven, I tried to tell people here on Earth about the teepees, but they couldn't understand what I was talking about. One day, some friends and I were on Mackinaw Island in Michigan. I saw teepees there. I told my friends, *"Oh my God, these teepees look just like the ones I saw in heaven."*

Another area of Heaven had small, one-level ranch houses. Jesus told me that these people did a little more for His Kingdom and for others. He then showed me bigger ranch homes and colonial homes of different sizes. Again, He explained that people obtained these homes because they had done more for His Kingdom and for people while they lived on Earth. Jesus then led me to a large community with many mansions. The mansions were enormous; much bigger than any mansion I have ever seen on Earth. The construction was of materials I can't find the words to describe. The mansions were so beautiful.

Then, Jesus asked me a question that left me speechless: *"Do you want to see your mansion?"*

I looked at Him and said, *"Oh, but Jesus, I haven't done anything for You on Earth yet."* He replied, *"I know, but you will."* Jesus took me to my mansion; I only saw the outside; it was spectacular. I saw people coming in and out of their mansions. Every mansion is different, and they are custom-made for each person. I started to recognize people from Earth. Then Jesus showed me Kenneth and Gloria Copeland coming out of their mansion. My mansion was right next to theirs. I thought, *"but they are still on Earth. How come they are here?"* Jesus knew my thoughts and answered my question. He said, *"Haven't you read Ephesians 2:6? The spirit can go back* and

forth between Earth and Heaven. The natural body is limited to Earth."
Then Jesus took me to another community where I recognized people who were attending a church in Bloomfield Hills, Michigan. In fact, it was a church I had visited a few times, but the church was over an hour drive from my home. The beauty of that church was that the teaching was very practical, and the people were joyful, and living out the Word of God in their everyday lives. It was at this church that I saw people who were living according to the Bible. It occurred to me that the people in this church were taking the Word seriously in their everyday life and were therefore storing up rewards in heaven. Their subdivision was above average.

I was really surprised to see so many people in Heaven. For some reason, I thought there wouldn't be anyone in Heaven except God the Father, the Lord Jesus, the Holy Spirit, some angels, and maybe a few people. I don't know why I thought that way, because people are everywhere in Heaven, and it is a very busy place. It looked like a bustling international airport. Heaven receives people every minute of every day. Just think about how many born-again people and children die every minute. Can you imagine Heaven receiving all those people every day? I said to Jesus, *"I can't wait to tell everyone on Earth what's going on up here."* Jesus nodded and smiled.

All the people who had mansions looked as if they were thirty-three years old. They looked like they did when they were in their prime on Earth. But the people who had smaller spaces looked the same age as they did on Earth. These people understood salvation, received Christ as their Savior, and made it to Heaven but, that was it. In my mind I thought, *"I don't want to end up like them looking old. I want to look like those people in the big mansions."*

After Jesus showed me all the mansions and houses, He said,

"Now I want to show you how we praise and worship here." Jesus led me to see this road, where troops of angels lined up in perfect order, praising and worshiping God. It looked like a movie I had seen where military troops were marching in unison and no one was distracted.

All the troops of angels had their eyes fixed on a large golden globe above them, which was the presence and glory of God. None of them were distracted or looking around. They were in total unison, order, and focus. One troop of angels had their hands raised while the music was playing everywhere. Another troop clapped their hands in perfect unison. The other troops played different instruments while focusing on the globe. One troop played the guitar, another the trombone, another the trumpet, another the harp, and still another was playing a drum attached to their chests. Then I saw another troop of angels dancing.

Jesus had a huge smile on His face; He was so happy to show me these things. He said, *"Now, are you convinced about how we praise and worship in Heaven?"* I said, *"I had no idea. I am convinced."* I grabbed Jesus' arm tightly and excitedly said, *"When I return to Earth, I will tell everyone what's going on up here!"* I repeated it five or six times. Jesus smiled and I knew He believed me. After seeing all this, the Psalms I had read were coming alive to me.

"...Clap your hands, all you peoples! Shout to God with the voice of triumph!" (Psalm 47:1, NKJV).
"Make a joyful shout to the Lord, all you lands!" (Psalm 100:1, NKJV)
"Lift up your hands in the sanctuary and bless the Lord." (Psalm 134:2, NKJV)
"Praise Him with the sound of the trumpet; Praise Him with the lute

and harp! Praise Him with the timbrel and dance; Praise Him with the stringed instruments and flutes! Praise Him with loud cymbals; Praise Him with clashing cymbals! Let everything that has breath praise the Lord." (Psalm 150:3-6, NKJV)

I truly believe Jesus took me to Heaven, not because I am a special person, but because He knew how confused I was about praise and worship. I'm in awe of God's love for me in that He would go out of His way to take my spirit to Heaven, just to show me what is going on in Heaven.

Jesus knew that I had a hard time seeing people praising God with uplifted hands and clapping. I came from a Catholic and Mormon background where I never saw those emotions expressed. As a matter of fact, the first time I attended a charismatic church, I was offended by the hand-raising, clapping, dancing, and loud music. I was so appalled that I immediately ran out of the building to go home.

When I got to the car, I heard a little voice on the inside of me say, *"You drove an hour to get here. Why don't you go back and at least hear the message?"* So, I waited outside the charismatic church until the music stopped. Then I went inside.

That night, the pastor spoke on praise and worship and gave many Bible references. I wrote down the references, and when I returned home, I went straight to read every verse I had written down. I thought, *"Wow, all of this is in the Bible!"* Even though I read these things in the scripture, I still was not convinced that people should show their emotions like that. But when Jesus showed me how they worship in Heaven, I was fully persuaded.

As Jesus continued my tour of Heaven, I understood that God

wants us to have days Heaven on Earth. In Matthew 6:10 Jesus said, *"Your kingdom come Your will be done on Earth as it is in heaven"* (NKJV). In Heaven, people did many activities we do on Earth; adults taught small children, people cooked. I was amazed to see people walking around, conversing with each other, and laughing. It reminded me of my little town in Italy where I grew up. Everyone knew each other.

There was no self-ambition in Heaven. No one wanted to be better than another person. There was no stepping on one another to get ahead. There is only one ambition in Heaven: getting to the throne where God the Father resides. Everything is done in love and with joy. I saw children playing, laughing, and splashing water on each other. The angels were doing the same thing in a river that was crystal clear.

After Jesus showed me all this, He said, *"Now, you and I are going to have some fun."* He took me to a river. On the way I said, *"But Jesus, I don't know how to swim."* He chuckled and He kept on walking. As we entered the river, I could see through the clear blue water all the way to the bottom. As we continued to walk, I realized I was not sinking. Jesus reached down with both hands, cupped them together, and splashed water on me. I wanted to splash Him back, but I thought, *"I must have a reverence for Him. I cannot do to Him what he did to me,"* so, I refrained.

Jesus knew my thought, looked at me, and said, *"Go ahead! Do it. Have fun."* So, I reached down, grabbed a handful of water, and splashed Him. We laughed and giggled together. And I thought once again, *"I'm standing and playing in the water, and I'm not sinking."* After that, Jesus said, *"Now, we need to start walking back."* After He said that, I understood that we had to get back to the gate

I had entered where Jesus was waiting for me when I first arrived in Heaven.

Jesus walked me through the gate and took me outside the gate. I noticed a thick fog coming from an area far away that looked dark and cloudy. As we took a few more steps forward, I saw a big drop-off like a cliff that separated us from the other area. I asked Jesus, *"Oh! What is that?"*

Jesus replied, *"Don't even look there. You don't want to know what's going on there."*

I then understood it was hell. Jesus said, *"No one from here can go there, and no one from there can come here."*

At that time, I had no knowledge about what I was seeing. It was all new to me. I later found the Scriptures that confirmed what I had seen. In Luke 16:19-31, the story of the rich man and Lazarus, the scripture says that there is a deep cliff. In verse 26, He said, *"… Besides all this, between us and you there is a great gulf fixed, so that those who want to pass from here to you cannot, nor can those from there pass to us"* (NKJV). The passage reveals that Lazarus was alive after he died and was living in the glories of Heaven. The rich man was also alive after he died and was living in the torments of hell.

As Jesus and I spent our last few minutes together, He looked into my eyes and asked, *"Will you tell everyone on Earth what you've seen here in Heaven?"* With great excitement, I said, *"Oh yes, oh yes, I will."*

What impressed me was that while Jesus showed me things during this visit, I had been saying many times, *"O, I am going to tell everybody what's going on up here!"* And yet, in the very last minute, Jesus emphasized for me to look into His eyes and promise Him that I would tell everyone when I returned to Earth. I felt like Jesus was giving me an assignment. After I came back from Heaven, I understood John 6:58 (NLT), *"I am the true bread that came down from heaven. Anyone who eats this bread will not die as your ancestors did (even though they ate the manna) but will live forever."*

You see, those of us who are born again do not die. We simply move from a corruptible body into a celestial or spiritual body; that is what happened to me. One second I was in my natural body, and the next second I was in my spiritual body and I could fly. In no time at all, I went from the natural world to Heaven. My spiritual body had no limits. After this experience, I understood more clearly why I had seen certain people in Heaven who were still on Earth (Ephesians 2:6).

•••

When I returned from Heaven, I reentered my body through my mouth. I know this may sound gross and unbelievable. This is difficult to get our natural mind around, but many things in the supernatural world are challenging to our natural understanding. To understand spiritual things, we do it by faith. Nevertheless, this is what happened to me.

A special sense of Jesus' presence lingered with me for a few days.

When I realized I was in my natural body again, I thought, *"Wow! This is exactly how it must be when we die. One second, we're here... and the next second we're there. We simply exhale in the earthly realm and then inhale in the heavenly realm. Christians don't die, but simply move from one place to another—from Earth to Heaven."* I then understood that eternal life starts when we receive Jesus in our hearts, not when we get to Heaven. Also, it makes sense what Jesus said, and whoever lives and believes in Me shall never die. Do you believe this?" (John 11:26).

For those that remain behind, it is hard because they don't know what is going on in Heaven. Those that die in Christ don't think about Earth anymore. They don't experience any struggle when they leave this Earth. There was a time when I feared dying. I believe most people fear dying. Since seeing and experiencing Heaven, I no longer fear, but have a great expectation of seeing it again!

This world does not compare with Heaven. Therefore, I wrote this book for many Christians that don't know what I know. When they lose a loved one who was a Christian, they don't have to despair because their loved one went to a better place. If you have lost a loved one, I hope this becomes comforting to you. You can stop grieving, knowing that your loved one is having a wonderful time in Heaven.

I can't take anything with me to Heaven except the people I help to get to know Jesus on Earth. For this reason, I willingly lay down my life so others can find life. This is where I find my purpose and joy and get my daily strength.

The next morning after my visit to Heaven, my kids and husband noticed something different in my countenance. I told them all that I saw in Heaven- the whole experience, and they were in awe! From that moment forward, everything I did came from a place of living for eternity. My passion became telling people about Jesus, and the encounters with Jesus continued.

CHAPTER EIGHT

God Changed My Name

After my visit to Heaven, I continued teaching my Italian and English Bible study groups and leading more and more people to Jesus. My passion for helping people increased even more. I was learning to apply God's Word to every situation I faced, and helping others do the same.

The work I did for God was all on a volunteer basis, so I continued to manage and build my apartment business to take care of my family and build investments for their future. There was little down time, and little time for recreation. I was driven to follow God wholeheartedly, but it was not easy. Amid many blessings, there were many challenges as well.

One Saturday morning during this time, I woke up from a terrible dream. The Lord would sometimes reveal things to me through dreams. This dream was strange to say the least. I dreamt that a monkey walked up to me while I was in bed. The monkey grabbed the edge of my mouth and aggressively pulled it back toward my ear. It felt like he was putting a clamp between my mouth and ear. The pain was excruciating.

When I woke up from the dream, my mouth and my ear were hurting. I tried to tell my family what happened, but my throat was in too much pain to talk. On Monday, I went to the doctor. The doctor asked, *"Why did you wait so long to come?"* I said, *"It has only been two days since I woke up like this."* The doctor continued, *"The growths on your throat are troubling, we will need to schedule surgery. So go home, and you must be on total voice rest for one week, no talking at all."* Since I did not know how to write English, this was a huge problem – how could I communicate with my children, who did not know how to read Italian?

Before I came to know Jesus, I would have fallen apart at this news. But with all I had been learning through reading the Bible and *The Believer's Authority* book by Kenneth E. Hagin, I thought, *"I will not go through surgery."* I started to do what I learned from the Word. I went home from the doctor's office. That same day took a pen and paper and wrote, *"whatever you are in my throat, I curse you and remove you from my throat, and cast you into the sea in Jesus' name. I believe that by Jesus's stripes I am healed."* I wrote this declaration again and again. Even though I was on voice rest, once in a while I would whisper the declaration. Most of the time, I just wrote it.

That same Monday during the night, I had another dream. In the dream, I saw my throat with two growths - each growth was about half the size of a boiled egg. The growths were touching each other. That was why I could not talk. I dreamt that every time I spoke that declaration, my words were forming bullets. Each time I declared those words, those bullets would hit the growths in my throat. As the bullets kept hitting the growths, they started loosening. The more I was saying those words, the more the growths loosened. Finally, they broke away from my throat and floated down through my body until they passed. That is how the dream ended.

After this dream, I woke up and realized that God was going to heal me. I thought, *"I don't have to declare anymore, because God is going to heal me anyway."* But then another thought came to me. I said, *"No, I am going to keep on whispering and writing, until I see my healing manifested."*

I am glad I did not stop making declarations, because the enemy did not stop his attack. A couple of days later, I was reading the Psalms when I heard a voice mocking me, saying, *"I got you; you're never going to talk again."* I knew this was a voice from the enemy.

I went right to the Bible and opened to 2 Corinthians 10:5. I pointed my finger at that verse and said this to the enemy, *"It is written. I bring every thought into captivity to the obedience of Christ."* This is why it is so important that we know the Word. When we get attacked, we do not have to struggle to find the prescription we need from the Word. I knew exactly where to go in the Bible.

A week had now passed since the Monday I went to the doctor. My appointment was scheduled at 4:00 PM. Around 2:00 PM, I was in the Psalms, reading the Bible, and I fell asleep. During my sleep, I had one of the most amazing dreams. In this dream, I was in a field all by myself. I looked and from afar, I saw a man coming toward me. I thought he might be an angel bringing me a message. I saw He was in linen robes with a big sash around his waist. As he came closer, I realized it was Jesus. He was walking toward me, and I started walking toward Him. In my mind, I was thinking to ask Him why He allowed this problem with my throat to happen to me.

When we were about four feet from each other, Jesus said, *"Sarah, beloved of God, the Lord is pleased with you. The Father and I love you so much, we are so pleased with you, we love what you are doing."*

Jesus was so excited to tell me this that He repeated the same thing several times.

I replied, *"First of all my name is Marie, not Sarah."* He then said, "But the Father and I call you Sarah!" So, I pointed to my throat and said, *"If you and the Father are so pleased with me, then why did you allow this to happen?"* Jesus did not answer me, He just put his left hand on my throat, and raised his right arm toward heaven and said, *"Father."* And I woke up from the dream.

Immediately I realized I could talk perfectly without pain. I knew I was healed. I yelled downstairs to my daughter, Tracy, who was watching soap operas, *"Tracy, Tracy! I'm healed!"* Tracy screamed from downstairs *"Don't talk, don't talk!"* I said, *"I can talk perfectly, it does not hurt!"* She ran upstairs and we both jumped up and down rejoicing that I was healed.

My doctor appointment was at 4:00 PM and my husband Mike came home to take me to the doctor. I told Mike I was healed but he said, *"I'm not going to go by dreams – we are going to the doctor."* When we saw the doctor, the doctor checked my throat and said, *"What happened? Everything is gone – your throat is perfectly clear!"* I told the doctor about my dreams. I asked if he could draw what my throat looked like when I came last week. He said yes. The doctor drew exactly what I had seen the Monday before in a dream after I had just started making declarations. His drawing looked like halves of a boiled egg touching each other in the middle of my throat. The doctor looked dumbfounded and said, *"Well, the only thing I can say is you have received a miracle."*

After the miracle, I kept thinking how in that dream, God had changed my name from Marie to Sarah. I told my children, *"I think I should change my name to Sarah, like the Father and Jesus call me. I* said, *"I read in the Bible how God changed names like Simon to Peter, and Saul to Paul."* I felt privileged that God would change my name like the people in the Bible. I said, *"I want to be obedient to God"* They said, *"Don't embarrass us by changing your name."* So, I put that on hold for many years

Ten years later, I went to a conference. The first night I was there, I was leaving the conference to go to my hotel. My daughter Tracy, her husband James, and my son Dino were all with me. A black woman was sitting next to me, and as I stood up to leave, she said, *"Sister, before you leave, I have a word for you."* She started prophesying over me. She said many things that God had already told me. I was amazed because this lady did not know me. How could she know all about me?

I recall some specific things she said, *"Sister, the Lord is so pleased with you. What is your name?"* I said, *"Marie."* She said, *"The Father calls you Sarah."* She continued, *"The Lord will use you tremendously, I see you speaking in a stadium."* Tracy, James, and Dino heard it as well. On the way to the hotel, we were all amazed that this lady knew all about me, when I had never seen her before. I realized that after ten years, God had not changed His mind. I thought, *"God still wants me to change my name from Marie to Sarah."* I asked my children, and I got the same response as before. So I postponed it again, because I did not want to bring conflict in the family by changing my name publicly.

In 2011, when I moved from Michigan to become a resident of Florida, I thought, *"this is the perfect time to change my name to Sarah."* My children were all still in Michigan, and I changed my name to Sarah.

CHAPTER NINE

Hearing and Following God's Voice

Since the time I read *The Believer's Authority* book by Kenneth E. Hagin, I began my search to find a church that would teach me like that book. In the meantime, I constantly and consistently kept reading the Bible. From the time I was saved, it took me three years to find the right church. Let me tell you how that happened.

One Saturday at 11 o'clock in the morning, I heard God tell me with urgency to go see a man called Tony Churece. I lived on the east side of Detroit and attended the Mormon church on the east side. Tony lived on the west side of Detroit and was a minister at the Mormon church on the west side. We would see him once a year when all the Mormons went to a conference in Pennsylvania, but I only knew him as an acquaintance.

I called Tony, and he said, *"Come on over."* I did not want to drive one hour away by myself, so I asked my husband Mike to take me there. Mike did not want to take me. He said, *"I am embarrassed. What are you going to tell him? That you hear voices?"* I said, *"If you don't want to take me, I will call somebody else to take me."* When he heard that I was going to call somebody else, he became curious of my urgency to see Tony and said, *"All right, I will take you."*

When we arrived a little after noon, we noticed that every window shade was down. When we walked in, the whole house was dark. Tony asked Mike, *"Why did you guys come here?"* Mike answered, *"I don't know why we are here. She hears voices and the voice told her to urgently come and see you."* Tony then grabbed me, put his head on my shoulder and started hugging me and crying uncontrollably.

I let him cry for a while, then he finally lifted his head off my shoulder, and I looked in his eyes and said, *"Now, you tell me why I am here."* Tony said, *"My wife is in California; she went to her brother's funeral. Her brother was a young man who died of cancer."* Then he said, "My father-in-law died of cancer. My sister died of cancer. I am surrounded by death. I can't handle this life anymore." Then he said, *"Just before your phone call, I was about ready to kill myself. I had my gun pointed into my ear. When the phone rang, it startled me, and I put the gun down. I thought I will take this call, then do it later. When I heard your voice, I was taken back because you never called me before and had never come to see me, and I wondered why you wanted to come over."*

Then Tony said, *"you said that you heard God's voice. I know you didn't learn how to hear God's voice in the Mormon church, where have you learned to do so?"* I said, *"I read the Bible cover to cover and after reading the Bible, I began to hear God's voice."* Mike said, *"That's all she does is read the Bible."*

Tony was amazed that God would care for him so much that He would tell me to call him.

Because of the way God used me to call him and visit him, Tony realized that God stopped him from killing himself. Mike and I saw Tony's countenance change and he look normal.

Tony said, *"I am so confused. Our Mormon church is supposed to be the only church that has the truth, but we never get anybody visiting our church. Recently, somebody invited me to visit their church. There was a young punk over there preaching from a book written by Kenneth E. Hagin, The Believer's Authority. That church is growing in numbers, and they get many professional people."*

When I heard that the pastor was teaching from *The Believer's Authority*, I remembered the prayer I had prayed to find a church that would teach me like that book. I made a mental note to go and visit that church. I asked Tony, *"Where is this church located?"* To my surprise, that church was meeting in an elementary school where my kids had attended, so of course, I knew where it was located.

As we were returning home from visiting Tony, I was thinking, *"Wow, God did it again! Tony received a miracle and did not commit suicide, and through Tony, I think I found the church I have been searching for over three years. God did a miracle for Tony and a miracle for me."* This is how God works. When Pat Robertson of the 700 Club heard God's voice, my life was spared. When I heard God's voice, Tony's life was spared. Years later, when I was on television for five years, we heard many testimonies of how people were watching my program, and were about to commit suicide, and changed their mind.

I visited that church. The church was called Believers Faith Fellowship. As I was walking in the parking lot, there were two girls playing. The younger girl fell and scraped her knee. She was crying and screaming. The older one laid her hands on the younger girl and said, *"No complication will come out of this fall. And pain go away, in Jesus' name."* After the prayer, the younger girl stopped crying and started playing again. I said, *"Wow, even the children know how to pray in this church.*" I knew I had found my church.

CHAPTER TEN

Every Miracle Begins With a Problem

My church, Believer's Faith Fellowship, became family to me. The pastor taught the Word of God in such a practical way. I was not only listening, but I was also doing the Word, applying it in my life consistently. But that did not mean my life was without challenges. The strife at home with my husband grew worse because I had drifted away from the Mormon church. He was furious that I was reading the Bible and growing in my faith.

One night I went to Bloomfield Hills Christian Church with my friend Finella to hear a guest speaker. The church was over an hour away from my home. On the way home as we were driving, it was snowing. Finella was driving. Suddenly, a bolt of lightning landed right on the hood of the car. We had no idea what was happening, because when it snows, you don't see lighting. We both said, *"What was that?"* Right after we said that I started speaking in tongues. Finella said, *"You just spoke in tongues"*. For so long I had wanted to receive the baptism in the Holy Spirit. That night I received it, and I was ecstatic. I had been wanting to receive it for so long and now I was so full of joy. I had no idea what I was about to face.

When I arrived home, I wondered why everything inside the home looked dark. As I walked in, I said to myself, *"Oh, Mike is not home yet"*. Then I heard Mike clear his throat. I said, *"Oh I thought no one was home. Why are you in the dark?"* Mike shouted angrily, *"Leave me alone!"* I had never heard him that angry, and I was afraid. So, I went right upstairs to bed. I laid in bed holding my Bible to my chest and was repeatedly saying, *"God, help me."* Mike came upstairs, he took the Bible from me, and threw it at the wall. He said, *"You can't waste the rest of your life reading that book!"*

Then, Mike went to my clothes closet, took every piece of clothing from my closet, and made a pile in the middle of the bedroom floor. Then Mike ran out of the room and down the stairs, taking the steps two at a time. I had never seen him this angry. I was frightened for my life.

Mike came back up the stairs, a couple steps at a time, and went in his closet, and did the same thing with his clothes. He put all his clothes in the middle of the floor. I had no idea why he was doing this. Then he ran out of the room, slamming the door so hard that the door jamb cracked. I thought, *"He is going to kill me tonight."* I had these thoughts that he would suffocate me with a pillow.

So, I began to say in my mind, Lord, protect me from this danger. I was exhausted and didn't know if I was going to fall asleep or not. So, I stacked many books behind the door so I would hear the books fall if he tried to get back into the room. I woke up in the morning and thankfully, nothing bad had happened overnight.

That morning, I started making Mike his favorite breakfast to show him that it did not matter what he did the night before, and he said, *"Why are you making breakfast for me?"* I said, *"I just wanted to bless you."* Mike said, *"I want you to know that you are alive by a miracle, because last night I was hearing these voices in my head that said, 'kill her, kill her'.* " Mike continued, *"but, I was exhausted and fell asleep on the couch."* When I heard that, I knew I could not stay in that house anymore. I did not know when the devil would tempt him again.

I called my son, Anton, who was at college in Tulsa, Oklahoma, and told him what had happened. Anton flew home right away. Mike had to be out of town that weekend. Anton moved me from my big mansion to live in a two-bedroom apartment, where I could be safe. In that little apartment, I experienced God more and more. I felt safe. Every day I came home from work managing the apartments, I was never afraid, but had peace. God made Himself so real to me and I had many encounters with Him there.

One morning I was praying, and then I knelt on the floor. I placed my head toward the ground in reverence. Right there, in that position, I saw two feet – right there – on the floor in front of me. I knew these were the feet of Jesus. I did not know that if I looked up, I might see all of Jesus. I kept my eyes fixed on His feet, in worship, in awe of Him. This is the kind of reality of God's presence I was experiencing more and more. Even though my marriage to Mike was in disarray and I was no longer living in a big mansion but in a two-bedroom apartment, God was sustaining and strengthening me, and helping me come to know the reality of walking supernaturally with Him.

After I was born again, I heard a pastor on the radio, named Clarence King. Because Clarence pastored in the same city in which I lived, I paid particular attention to what he had to say. Pastor Clarence testified that when he started his church, his congregation was very small, and the finances were tight. Clarence really enjoyed coffee, but he thought that coffee was a luxury, not a necessity. He prayed and said to the Lord, "*I know that coffee is not a necessity, but I really like coffee.*" Clarence continued, "*I'm going to buy a can of coffee and I'm expecting you to multiply it.*" So, Clarence bought a can of coffee and every time he made coffee, he made the coffee without looking directly into the coffee can. And one can of coffee lasted him seven months. When I heard this testimony, I said, "*Oh, God multiplied that coffee for him.*" That testimony really built my faith in God.

Now, in my little apartment, I found myself in a similar situation as Pastor Clarence. I remembered his testimony and I applied that same principal. This is how my testimony goes. My husband, Mike, took my name off our bank account and charge card. When I found out, I called my attorney. The attorney said it would take three to four months to straighten this up.

When I heard this, I thought, I have wealthy friends. I can borrow money from them and when all this gets straightened up, I can pay them back. But I heard God's voice from within me, say, "*I don't want you to talk about this situation to anyone, not even your children. You must trust me.*" I only had $50 in my purse. But I remembered the testimony Pastor Clarence King gave on the radio about how God multiplied his coffee. I took my $50 and put it under the mattress. Each time I needed some money to buy groceries, I reached under the mattress with my eyes closed, and pulled out some money. And that $50 lasted for three months. God became my source for three months.

I totally relied on God because He had given me specific instruction to not tell anyone about what Mike had done to cut me off financially. I obeyed what God told me and God did his part by multiplying my last $50. On the very day the attorney called to inform me that I could use my bank account and credit card again, I went to reach for money under the mattress, and there was no more money.

Later when I faced other challenges, I would think of this experience and say to myself, *"as God was faithful then He will be faithful to me again"*. God met all my needs, not according to the natural, but He supernaturally met my needs. I am abundantly supplied more than I ever thought or even imagined.

I started to put my faith out there for things in my life that I would have previously never thought God was interested in helping me solve. I used to think that I had to fend for myself through all the inconveniences that came my way. One such experience, I well recall.

I was going to visit my children who were in college at Oral Roberts University in Tulsa, Oklahoma. My daughter, Tracy, had made plans for me to attend a conference and do some other activities with Christian women. It was the time of the month when I was going to have my menstrual cycle. I prayed and believed that God would intervene so I would not have to be inconvenienced during my stay in Tulsa. I had faith that this could be delayed until I returned.

I arrived in Tulsa and for the next ten days, I had a wonderful time with no inconvenience from my normal menstrual cycle. When I left Tulsa to return to my apartment in Michigan, my daughter took me to the airport. She asked me, *"Who is going to pick you up at the airport in Detroit?"* I said, *"I don't know, but God will provide."*

As I got on the plane, I sat next to a woman. She looked very sad, and I did not know how to approach her. Finally, I got the nerve to say, *"I'm noticing that you're sad, can I help you? I'm a Christian"* but she said, *"no, I'm not sad."* So I started reading a book that I had bought in Tulsa by Oral Roberts, and the book was titled, *Intended for Pleasure.* That book talked about that you could have a marriage from which you experience pleasure.

The woman was glancing at my book as I was reading, and she asked me, *"Where did you get that book?"* I told her where I had purchased it. I said, "If you want to read this book, I could lend it to you."

She said, *"Would you do that?"* She was taken back that I would do that. I said, *"Where do you live?"* She told me where she lived - right around the apartment where I lived. I said to her, *"Oh, who's picking you up?"* She said, *"No one. I left my car at the airport and I'm just going to pick up my car and go home."* I said, *"I live right around the block from your home. Will you give me a ride home?"* She said, *"Of course."* She took me home and she even took my suitcase upstairs to my apartment.

As I opened the door, my menstrual cycle immediately began. When I realized what was happening, I started rejoicing and screamed, *"Oh God! You did it exactly how I asked!"* The woman didn't understand why I was so happy and joyful but when I explained it to her, she was so stirred up and we talked about how God is so good. After she heard what God had done for me, she wanted to know more about God.

At the time when I had told my daughter that God would provide a ride home from the airport, I believed God would do it. And God did it by sitting me on the plane right next to this woman who lived a street over from where I lived.

Many people wouldn't even think to ask God for help with simple life problems. That was the mentality that I had before I came to know the Word. I didn't think it was practical to bother God for those little things, but I became fully persuaded that God wanted to get involved with me and everything in my life. That is why I asked him for a delay in my menstrual cycle – to make the time in Tulsa with my children and activities easier, and He did it for me!

By telling you these experiences, I hope to encourage you that God will get involved with your day-to-day life and needs. He is with you in everything. I believed that God would get involved and change my body around. When I finally discovered that God could and would work even in situations like this, I felt I had a best friend living with me all the time. These are the kinds of things that God did while I was living in that apartment. I was experiencing God so much that I did not at all miss the big mansion that I had left behind with all the fancy furniture and luxury.

I was in that two-bedroom apartment for about a year and a half. Mike had been doing mission work in Argentina. One day, I received a call from one of Mike's cousins, Carmela Zasa, who called me from Argentina. When Carmela was in Italy, she was my next-door neighbor growing up. Carmela had married one of Mike's cousins and moved to Argentina. Carmela called me to tell me that she had seen Mike and this other woman being romantic. I then knew divorce was inevitable for Mike and I. Strangely, I was happy for him. When Mike returned from Argentina, our divorce process started.

I didn't want to lose any part of my wealth during the divorce. I was advised that the lawyers would end up with more money than Mike and I and my concern was that my children would lose that part of their inheritance. So, while I was driving one day I asked God, *"God, what do I do?"* I heard God say, *"Go into partnership with Mike; don't divide the properties."* I thought, *"partner with him?"* I didn't want to partner with him. We were in the process of divorce!

Well, after I decided to listen and follow what God advised, I mentioned it to Mike. He said, *"No way!"* I went to the bank and told the vice president I thought it would be best to partner with my husband, but Mike didn't want to be in partnership with me. The vice president said, *"That is the best idea, because the lawyers would end up with more money than both of you."* Then, the vice president said, *"Let me talk to Mike."* The vice president called Mike and convinced him that a partnership would be better for both of us. I could not convince him, but the vice president did.

Mike continued to travel and do missions full time. I managed the apartment business myself. As a result, God opened more opportunities to buy more multifamily properties, and the business grew quickly from 250 apartments to 457 apartments.

God guided me through the divorce process. He provided the right people to help me. God gave me the insight on how to walk through my divorce with God at my side. The result was that our entire family's wealth was greatly increased, and nothing was lost. Only God can take an impossible mess and turn it into a miracle.

CHAPTER ELEVEN

Desiring God's Glory

One Wednesday night at Believer's Faith Fellowship church, Rick Tidwell, my pastor at that time, taught about the glory of God and how Moses had seen the glory of God. Yet, Moses wanted more of God's glory. The way Pastor Rick told the story was so real to me. I was so affected by the message that before I went to bed that night, I knelt and said to God, *"you have shown your glory to Moses, and then Moses wanted to see more of your glory. Lord, you said in your word that you are not partial. What you do for one you'll do for another. Show me your glory. Come in the night season. You said ask, and I am asking right now."*

Then I fell asleep with an expectation that something supernatural was going to happen during the night. I thought I would have an exceptional dream but when I woke up at 6:00 AM, nothing had happened, no dream, no visitation. I sat up in bed holding my Bible and said, *"Father, you said, ask and it shall be given. Well, I have asked. So, if you don't want to show me your glory, what can I do?"*

Right after I said that I heard a voice from behind me and the voice said, *"if you strip yourself of any fleshly desire and put on Christ, you will see my glory.*" I answered and said, "*how do I do that?*" The voice answered back to me and said, "How did you get saved? You believed in your heart, and spoke words with your mouth, and you got saved." I answered, "*It is that easy?*" I started to say, "*I strip myself of any fleshly desires and I put on Christ.*" Before I could even finish the word, "Christ", Jesus appeared standing in the air. His head was a foot lower than the ceiling.

Jesus and I started conversing mind to mind. He was not talking audibly, and I was not talking audibly. He was quoting scriptures and I was quoting scriptures. I thought, "*the Bible is God's language.*" Our conversation was based on the Word of God. I then understood why it is so important to know the Word of God. It's Jesus' language also. We were having so much fun I said to Jesus, "*Oh my, this is what it means to have the mind of Christ!*"

As I was conversing with Jesus, out of nowhere, there appeared a physically attractive man about six foot tall, wearing overall jeans. He stood between Jesus and me. This man started speaking audibly to me, just like people normally talk in the natural. The man said, "*Don't listen to Him, (referring to Jesus), but listen to me, and if you listen to me, I will give you all this*" and he extended his hand to show me what he wanted to give me.

He showed me my property I had in Roseville, Michigan. It consisted of 120 apartments and 15 buildings. And on the roof of those buildings, the roofs were full of gems, diamonds and gold, all glistening. Right before my eyes, the buildings kept on multiplying into many more buildings, and the buildings were multiplying so fast. He said, "*If you listen to me, and do what I say, I will give you all of what you see.*" I answered, "*What am I going to do with all that? I don't want all that, I want Him,*" and I pointed at Jesus.

Then the scene changed, and this man standing between Jesus and me showed me the property I owned in Pennsylvania. That property was also a 120-unit apartment complex with 15 buildings. He showed me, like before, that the roofs of the buildings were full of gems, diamonds, and gold, all glistening. Right before my eyes, the buildings kept on multiplying into many more buildings, and the buildings were multiplying so fast. I said, *"What am I going to do with all that? I don't want it. I want Him,"* and I pointed at Jesus.

I was aggravated because I felt like this man was distracting me from Jesus. As this continued, the man took me to a building where I had an exercise business. He showed me the roof – again, I saw the roof of that building full of gems, diamonds and gold, all glistening. Right before my eyes, the building kept on multiplying so fast, like a chain of buildings. He said, *"You can have all of that."*

I became upset at this man, and raised my voice to him, saying like I told him before, *"What am I going to do with all that? I don't want it. You can have it, I want Him,"* as I pointed at Jesus. The man became angry, and spit at me. It was a thick mucus and it landed right on my chest. I took a deep breath and blew that mucus off my chest, and it went flying into his face. When I did that, I thought, *"he is going to get even more angry."*

Instead, he gazed at me intensely. It was so strange. I felt like I was being hypnotized. I began to feel weak, like I was losing my strength. When this started to happen, I was a little cocky with him knowing that Jesus was right there and thinking Jesus was going to help me. I became weaker and weaker. I then realized that this was not a mere man, this was something demonic.

I looked up at Jesus and mind to mind I said, *"Jesus, aren't you going to help me?"* Jesus said, *"I can't. YOU need to say, 'It is written, be gone from me!'"* To my surprise, with Jesus I could speak mind to mind, but with this demonic person I had to speak words. I said to that man, *"It is written, be go…"* I never finished the word "gone" when he transformed right before my eyes. He went from a physically attractive man to a brutally ugly beast. The beast began to screech and edge himself backward, then he said, *"I'm leaving for a while, but I will be back."* He vanished. So now, I was with only Jesus again. Jesus said, *"if you would not have resisted the devil by saying, 'it is written, be gone from me', I could not have resisted the devil for you, because YOU have the authority to resist him!"* The experience ended.

In the beginning of this experience, the voice told me, *"If you strip yourself of any fleshly desire, you will always see my glory."* This sounds so easy. Just strip yourself and Jesus will be there. I tried to do the same thing other times, but Jesus did not appear to me each time. Then I understood that it had to be a way of life. I had to keep it before me, not to give in to selfish desires. When we give into our own selfish agenda, like desiring wealth, fame or anything that distracts us from Jesus, we give place to the devil to come around and take advantage of us.

Jesus said, *"For what profit is it to a man if he gains the whole world, and loses his own soul? Or what will a man give in exchange for his soul?"* (Matthew 16:26). If we gain the whole world for 100 years or so, and lose out on being with God for all eternity, what good is it?

CHAPTER TWELVE

Guidance and Protection for Our Family

God has divinely guided my family through many challenges and decisions through the years. For example, my eldest son Anton was in a valley of decision, my second son Dino was faced with a dangerous situation, and my daughter Tracy was at death's door. In each situation, God came through in a miraculous way. I want to build your faith to believe for God's guidance in your family as well.

For many years, I have prayed Isaiah 54:13 over my children. *"All your children shall be taught by the Lord, and great shall be the peace of your children"* (NKJV). This is the way I pray it, *"My children are taught of the Lord, and great is their peace."* I encourage you to pray the Word over your family.

ANTON'S STORY

After my first son Anton graduated from high school, he shocked me with an announcement. Anton told me that he and two of his buddies made plans to move to California, away from our home in Michigan. Without me knowing, my son made plans to move across the country. It never crossed my mind that he would make such a radical decision because he was happy and enjoyed living with our family. We used to worship and pray together every morning.

All three of my children were eager to learn about the Lord from me because they saw my relationship with the Lord, and they desired the same kind of relationship with the Lord. I never sensed any discontentment. Therefore, I was so shocked when Anton told me about his plan because this was not like him. He did not have a meaningful plan for college or employment. He was just relocating to California to be with his friends.

While I wanted my son's happiness and success, I was deeply concerned for him. I had an awareness inside of me that was very disturbing; I felt strongly that if my son moved to California, I would never see him again and because of that strong awareness, I did not want him to go. I tried to talk to him, but he would not even give me a chance to hear me out. He said, *"Mom, don't even try to change my mind, and don't try to stop me, I am going to California."*

I took my concern to God. I said, *"Lord, you see that I cannot reason with my son, but I know you alone can make a way where there seems to be no way. I don't know how to handle this situation, but nothing is too difficult for you. My son is more your son than mine because Anton is mine only while I live on earth. He is yours for now and all eternity."* Then I prayed in the Spirit, and I had an expectation that God was going to do a miracle. I did not tell anyone about my concern or how I had prayed. I never went into worry, because I knew enough to know that worry would only paralyze me. But my concern led me to action. My actions were to pray and intercede.

A week before Anton was leaving for California, he had a dream. In that dream, he saw himself in our home, in the dining room.

There was a large sliding door wall from which you could see outside. At the sliding door wall, on the outer side of the glass, there was a bird. The bird was pecking at the window. Anton was annoyed by this bird. He went to the door wall and moved his arms to scare the bird away, but the bird would not move. It just kept pecking on the window. So, Anton opened the door wall to try to shoo the bird away. As Anton did that, the bird dropped a piece of paper in his hand, and then the bird flew away.

When Anton opened that piece of paper, there was writing on it. The words said, *"Anton, don't go to California."* When Anton woke up from that dream, he knew that it was God telling him not to go to California. I was downstairs, and I heard Anton screaming from his upstairs bedroom, *"Mom, mom, I am not going to California. God does not want me to go."*

He came downstairs in the kitchen where I was. He was shaking as he told me all the details of the dream. He was in awe that God would be that specific to tell him not to go to California. When I heard these things, immediately within my heart, I said, *"Lord, you are faithful to me. You are so faithful to me!"*

Anton's buddies went to California. Two years later, his buddies purchased motorcycles and they both died in an accident. Their mothers never saw their sons again. When I heard this, I felt so bad for those two boys and their families. It was then that the dream God had given to my son became clearer. I understood why God put that strong awareness and concern in me that if my son would have gone to California, I would never see him again.

As believers, we have the privilege of God showing us things to come. John 16:13 says *"However, when He, the Spirit of truth, has come, He will guide you into all truth; for He will not speak on His own authority, but whatever He hears He will speak; and He will tell you things to come."* What a privilege we have in Jesus, that the God who rules the universe gets involved in our daily lives.

Hearing God's voice is the most profitable thing for us while we live in this life. Sometimes we get a warning, like in this testimony. Other times, it is a blessing that is coming our way. This is why it is important for us to stay in tune with the Holy Spirit.

DINO'S STORY

This is a story about how God protected my son, Dino.

It was a cold and rainy night in Michigan. I went to bed and wasn't aware that the rain was turning into ice. At 2:00 o'clock in the morning, I had a dream. In the dream, I saw a car accident happening – two cars crashing into each other. I saw my son Dino's head go through his car's windshield. His face had cuts all over and it was bleeding. I woke up terrified from that dream.

I felt that dream was a warning that my son Dino could be involved in a car accident in the future. To calm myself down, I started praying. "I take authority over what I saw in this dream, and I declare that no weapon that is formed against my son will prosper, in Jesus' name". Then I prayed in the Spirit until I felt peace. After I felt at peace, I went back to bed.

In the morning, my son Dino got up and went to school. As he was driving to school, the roads had iced over and what I saw in my dream happened. He was driving and could not stop. The other driver could not stop either and they crashed into each other.

The cars were both totaled. My son's head went into his car's windshield, and the glass broke into pieces, but Dino's head and face were not scratched in the least. When I talked to Dino later, he explained that it felt like his head hit a pillow when he hit the windshield. The other driver was injured, but not seriously. It was absolutely a miracle that both drivers were not killed.

I was still sleeping when the police called me to tell me that my son was in a car accident. I didn't panic. Normally, I might have panicked, but because I had the dream and I had prayed, I remained calm. This taught me that when we go through things, God is with us going through it with us.

I knew the Holy Spirit directed me to pray and that my prayer spared my son's life. This is the privilege that we have as believers; that we can command bad things to pass us over. Jesus said, *"all authority has been given to me."* Now, you and I have that same authority. Go ahead and use it in Jesus' name!

TRACY'S STORY

In the Old Testament, it was only the prophets or occasionally kings who would hear God's voice. In the New Testament, because the Holy Spirit lives in every believer, every believer can hear from God. Let me remind you that John 16:13 says, *"However, when He, the Spirit of truth, has come, He will guide you into all truth; for He will not speak on His own authority, but whatever He hears He will speak; and He will tell you things to come."*

When my daughter, Tracy, was 21 years old, she was dating this young man, Marcus, from Boston. Everything was going so well. In the midst of this joyous time, I had a dream that Tracy was very sick. I saw her laying in a coffin, dead. I woke up from that dream. I said, *"No weapon formed against my daughter can prosper (Isaiah 54:17)."* I did not pray about it anymore and since everything was going so well, I did not think about it anymore.

A year later, Tracy had been married to Marcus and living in Boston with her in-laws. I was in Michigan. One morning, I was getting ready to go to church as usual, putting my makeup on, and I had a sense that a spirit of death was surrounding my daughter Tracy. I felt she was very sick. Right away, I called Tracy in Boston. Tracy did not answer.

I immediately called Tracy's mother-in-law. I said, *"Lynn what is happening to my daughter? I had an awareness that she was dying."* Lynn said, *"Oh my, you are right! The Lord revealed it to you. Tracy was not able to breath, and now she is in the ambulance on the way to the hospital. I was just closing the door to follow the ambulance when I heard the phone. I went back to the kitchen to answer the phone. I have to go; I will call you later, pray!"*

When I heard what Lynn said, I started screaming at the spirit of death. I said, *"spirit of death, Jesus gave me authority over you! Jesus said you must obey me. Leave my daughter's body, in Jesus' name!"* I started declaring, *"The law of the spirit of life in Christ Jesus has made my Tracy free from the law of sin and death!"* (Romans 8:2). *"Tracy will live and not die!"* As I said this repeatedly, the gift of faith came from within. I knew that the spirit of death had left her, and Tracy was going to be fine.

By the time Tracy arrived at the hospital, she was breathing normally. The doctors found nothing wrong with her. In the dream I had a year before, God was trying to warn me about this situation with Tracy that was coming. I realized that I should have taken the time to intercede when I had that dream to stop the devil's plan. This was a real-life lesson for me. Also, had I not learned how to have this kind of relationship with God, I would not have had the awareness that death was surrounding my daughter, and she could have died. I would not have had the joy of having three beautiful granddaughters from Tracy. God tells us about many things in His Word. If we do not pay attention, we do not profit ourselves and the people we love.

CHAPTER THIRTEEN

Starting The Churches - The Ripple Effect

Romans 5:8 says, *"But God demonstrates His own love toward us, in that while we were still sinners, Christ died for us."* (NKJV) While I was still a sinner, God prepared a "winning" plan for me.

About a year after we started Life Christian Church, we received a call from the 700 Club. They wanted to record a program to talk about how I was saved through their television program. Till this day, I still do not know who let the 700 Club know that I was saved through their ministry and that years later, I had started a church.

When they put the program together, they said that the impact of my decision to come to Christ would have a ripple effect through other people that would connect with my ministry. When you drop an object into water, ripples expand outwards. The impact grows larger and larger across the water. Those ripple effects are continuing through the lives of people touched by our churches through the years. Everyone is a part of those ripples because their lives will affect others. Our churches were started supernaturally. God didn't call us to just make a dent in one location. He called us to make a difference in all the locations we were in.

So, how did this ripple effect begin? As I previously talked about, I found *The Believer's Authority* book by Kenneth E. Hagin. Then I found a church where the pastor had gone to Bro. Hagin's Rhema Bible College, so he was teaching along the same line as Bro. Hagin. I was very selective in whose teaching I was hearing. I would only hear faith teachers.

I was in Believer's Faith Fellowship church for one year. I was scheduled to go to Italy to see my family. I had heard on the radio about an "Italians for Jesus" Bible study. I went to visit the Bible study to see if they had literature in Italian to take to my family in Italy. When I got there, I found twenty-five Catholic women. I grew up Catholic, so I knew where these women were coming from.

I was under the impression that the Bible study had been going for a long time, but when I visited, I discovered they had just started two weeks before. The teacher had to help each person, one at a time, find the chapter and verse because they did not know how to find chapters and verses in the Bible. I thought, *"Oh, wow, this teacher and these people need help."* I went back each week, not to learn, but to help the women open their Bibles and find the verses.

Three months later that teacher's job transferred him to Arizona. The women saw that I cared about them and wanted to help them, so they asked me if I would be their teacher. I went to my pastor at Believer's Faith Fellowship and told him that the Italian people wanted me to teach them. The pastor laid his hands on my head and said, *"You are ready. Go and preach the good news and God will be with you."*

I loved what my pastor was preaching on Sunday so much, that whatever I heard on Sunday, I passed on to the group at the Tuesday Bible study. The Bible study grew, and we had to move from the house to the Italian Cultural Center. The people were growing spiritually, and the Italian group grew to forty-five.

A woman by the name of Rosa Andairi brought her mother to the Italian Bible study, because her mother only spoke and understood Italian. Rosa understood Italian but could not speak it. So, Rosa said to me, *"This message must be heard in English. Come to my house and give the same message to my friends."* I said, *"English? I want you to know, I cannot pronounce certain words right in English."* Rosa said, *"No, I will sit next to you and the words that you do not pronounce right, I will pronounce for you. But I want my friends to hear this message."*

I went to Rosa's home one Sunday afternoon and she had fifteen English-speaking Catholic women there. I thought I would find three to four people there, to my surprise there were fifteen. Those women had never heard the things I was telling them. The message I was giving to the Italian Bible study, I started giving to the English group. And the English Bible study grew so fast that soon it had to move from Rosa's house to Paulette Chambers' finished basement. When the basement got full, Paulette's husband started complaining. He said, *"I thought this Bible study was just going to be a few people. But this is a zoo! And the street is full of cars. Soon the neighbors are going to complain."* Paulette's husband said we could not use the basement any longer.

Most of the people in this Bible study were living right around my home. There was a church a mile away from my home. So, I went to ask the pastor if I could use a room in his church for my Bible study. That pastor gave us a room to meet. After 8 months at this church, God said to me, *"It's time to move from the church to Shelby Nursing Home – they will give you a room."* This nursing home was right across the boulevard from the church in which we had been meeting.

So, I called a friend of mine. She lived a mile away from me. Her name was Fran.

I told Fran what God said and that I was so excited about God giving us direction. Fran said, *"Don't go to Shelby Nursing Home until I get there. I want to see this miracle!"* Fran came to pick me up and as we were driving to Shelby Nursing Home, I heard God say, *"Don't tell them it's a Bible study, they won't give you the room".* I said to Fran, *"Uh-oh! God just told me not to tell them this is a Bible study, but God did not tell me what to say."* Fran said, *"Well, I don't know what to tell you, God talks to you, He's not talking to me!"*

Then I had a thought, *"If I don't know what to say, I should go back home until God tells me what to say."* Then I had another thought, *"God will give me the words to say."* So, we continued driving in the car to the nursing home. When we arrived, we talked to the secretary at the desk. We told her that we needed a room to teach a group of people. The secretary said, *"What are you teaching them?"* And without thinking, these words came out of my mouth, "I teach people how to be overcomers." She said, *"Oh, I like that. We could use more overcomers in this country."* So, she took me to see the room. The room was so big. It even had a microphone and speaker system, and a little pulpit. She said, *"You don't have to do a thing. We will prepare the chairs for you. You just show up."*

I was so happy that the secretary did not ask me if this is a Bible study. I thought, *"thank God, she did not ask me."* As Fran and I were walking toward the door to leave, the secretary called us back. She said, "This is not a Bible study, is it?" I said, *"Well, I take a verse or two from the Bible, and then I build on it."* She said, *"Oh, okay."* So as Fran and I were ready to leave for a second time, the secretary called us back again and said, "*And one condition, that I need to attend at least one time. I can't come all the time because I'm working. But I want to come once.*" I said, "*Oh, sure, come.*" When she came, she liked it so much that she began to tell everyone who came to visit the nursing home. She became my biggest promoter, and the group grew.

At that nursing home, we grew to over one hundred people. Soon, the people were starting to put pressure on me to start a church. I didn't want to start a church. First because I am a woman and most people want to hear from a man, and second, I was divorced. I looked at all the odds against me. In the natural, I feared what the people would say. God was telling me, "*Don't pay attention to what the people think.*" But I was taking my time, putting off starting a church. I was waiting for a lightning bolt from heaven to tell me to start a church.

In the meantime, I went to Israel for ten days. I left my son, Anton, to take care of the Bible study for the ten days I was gone. The very last night in Israel before I was leaving to go home, the preacher said, "*I want to lay hands on any pastor or minister who teaches Sunday School, or a Bible study. If that is you, come to the front.*" Well, so many people rushed to the front. Both men and women were climbing over the chairs to get to the front. I was surprised to see most of the people going forward. I started to go, but when I saw the chaos, I stopped and thought, "*I do not want to be trampled.*"

I closed my eyes and started talking to God, "*Well, Lord, I wanted to go to the front, but you see what is going on, you can touch me right here.*" When I said that, a hand touched my shoulder and I screamed because it startled me. When I opened my eyes, I saw this lady who had put her hand on my shoulder. She was screaming, *"I found you, I found you. Thank God, I found you!"* She was so excited. I thought, *"Who is this cuckoo?"*

She noticed I was skeptical to see her that excited and she said, *"I know you are startled, and I know you don't understand my excitement. Sister, listen to me. I am from Missouri. I was in my living room and God gave me a vision. I saw your face and your height."* God gave me a message to give to you. God said, *"I want you to go to Israel because you are going to meet this woman you saw in the vision. I want you to tell her to start my church this year."*

She was crying, trembling, as she said, *"Sister, you must believe what I am telling you, because I did not have the money to come to Israel, but God provided. God touched someone's heart to pay for my trip and here I am because God wanted me to give this message to you. All the nine days I have been here, I was bewildered because, from the first day, I was looking for the person I saw in the vision. Every day it did not happen, I lost hope, because tomorrow morning we are leaving to go home. But then, on the very last night, He led me to you. If you would have run to the front like the others, I would not have seen you. God directed your steps and my steps – thank God!"*

When she said all this, I believed her, because God had been telling me all along to start a church. This was my lightning bolt of the confirmation I had been waiting for. I knew that God was in this. So, the journey began. We started the church in a storefront, then we moved into an elementary school. After a year, we moved into a high school. After another year, we bought a church building in Clawson, Michigan and later moved to Troy, Michigan.

After two years of that Troy church running, I moved into a new house in Rochester Hills, Michigan. One day, I was praying and telling God, *"Lord, I want to make a difference where I live in Rochester Hills. I want to be the little light for you here in Rochester Hills."* As I was praying, I heard God's voice from within my belly. God said, *"Not Rochester Hills yet. Go to Howell and start another church."* I only knew one couple, Ed Dombrowski, a builder, and his wife, who lived in Howell, Michigan. Ed had been attending my Bible study for a couple years, then he got busy with his building business. I had not seen him for a few years, but I had his phone number and called him.

I called Ed and said, "Will you help me start this church in Howell? Ed said, *"I am delighted to help you."* I said, *"Find me a school where we could meet. If you have any friends, ask them to come."* I took twenty people from our main campus church and my son, and we went to start the church in Howell. After a while, I left my son there to pastor that church and I went back to the main campus church.

A year after we started the Howell campus, I noticed a lady at our main campus who was coming from Algonac, which was over an hour drive one way to come to church. She had to be there early to set up for and to direct the Children's Ministry. So, you can imagine she had to leave her house very early on Sunday morning. My heart went out to her. By the time I got there on Sundays, she had already been at the church a long time. I would say to her, *"I totally appreciate what you are doing, Barbara Krajenke."*

My appreciation was so great, I was sympathizing that she was doing all this sacrifice. After a few months, I heard God say, *"If you really feel bad for her, why don't you bring the church to where she lives?"* After God told me that, I made an appointment with Barbara. I said to her, *"Do you want this church to come to your house in Algonac?"* She was so taken back, she said, *"What do you mean?"* I said, *"If you want it, you can have it. Here is what I want you to do; start a Bible study in your home. I will come and teach the people each week. When the Bible study grows to 25 people, I will bring a pastor and we will establish that Algonac campus church."* Barbara was faithful to make it happen, and her Bible study grew.

After a year of doing Bible studies in Barbara's home, where I was teaching them once a week and Barbara was cultivating the people all week long, being a friend, and encouraging them, Barbara found a Methodist church that let us hold our service in their building on Sunday afternoons. So, I brought a pastor with his wife, and we established the church there.

Two years later, we found and purchased a building in New Baltimore and the Algonac campus moved into that building. That is how that campus was established. A few people from Port Huron drove almost an hour to attend services in New Baltimore. Pastor Diane Shannon repeated the same process I had done in Algonac, asking the Port Huron group to begin a Bible study in Port Huron. In the meantime, Pastor Diane trained leaders to go and start the Port Huron campus. There was a church in Port Huron in the middle of a neighborhood that was empty. That is where the Port Huron campus church was established.

Four years later, there were forty people who had been meeting in a basement in Flint, Michigan. They called us and asked us if we could send a pastor and start a campus there. My son Dino and his wife went to start that campus church in Flint.

In 2011, God told me to move to Naples, Florida, but never told me why. I felt like Abraham, who did not know where he was going, but he obeyed. So, I obeyed and moved to Naples. I did not know even one person in Naples.

Two weeks later, a man came to rent an apartment right next to my apartment. I was sitting outside, and he started talking to me. Jeff said, *"Where are you from?"* I said, "Michigan." He said, *"What did you do in Michigan?"* I said, *"I had a business in Michigan, and I am the founding pastor of a few churches in Michigan."* He said, *"What are you doing in Naples?"* I said, *"If you are not a Christian, you are not going to understand."* He said, *"I am a Christian. I am Methodist, I teach Sunday School, so try me."* So, I told him how God directed me to come to Naples. He said, *"Oh, now I know why God told you to come to Naples. I have a friend, who is a pastor, whose wife left him a few weeks ago, and he is very depressed. He is having a hard time doing church. If you would help Him until he comes out of this depression, that would be wonderful."*

So, I gave Jeff my number and the next day, the pastor called me, we talked, and he asked me to help him. After a month, the pastor decided he wanted to stop doing church and get into business, so he gave the church to me to pastor. The fifty people I started with, had not been taught the message of faith. So, one of the first things I did was start talking to the people about faith and relationship with God. We had a Bible Institute in Michigan, so I brought the courses to Naples and gave the people one year of courses free of charge to establish them in the message of faith. Over the course of five years, the church grew to over 600. I gave that church to my daughter to pastor and that church continues.

Can you see the ripple effect? From the Italian Bible study to the English Bible study to a church, to another church, to another church. What kind of ripple effect do you want to see out of your life?

CHAPTER FOURTEEN

The Pear Tree

Four years before I had started the first church, I was leaving home in the morning for the business office. At the time, I was leading two Bible studies one in English, one in Italian and leading thirty-five women in the prayer ministry at Believer's Faith Fellowship church. For many years, I had taken the same route to work. This one morning, I felt like a nudge to take another route.

While I was driving, I saw this tree. From far away it looked like beautiful flowers on the tree. I had never seen a tree like that. When I got closer, I realized that the tree was not full of flowers, but it was full of pears. There were so many pears on that tree, they were red and green. I had never seen anything like it. I parked, got out the car, and went to look more closely at this tree. There were stakes underneath the branches so that the branches would not break under the weight of the pears. There were so many pears!

I knew there was a reason why God had changed my route that morning to lead me to that tree. As I stood in the front of the tree, I started to count the pears, but there were too many to count. I said, *"Lord, I cannot count all these pears, but you know how many pears there are on this tree. Give me this many spiritual children."* I felt like Abraham when he was counting the stars. So, for the whole season until there were no more pears on the tree, I stopped by this tree morning and night while saying the same thing: *"Thank you, Lord, that you have given me this many spiritual children."* I had learned to call things to be as though they were already.

God led me to this pear tree to give me a vision of how many spiritual children He wanted to give me. You see, many people receive a vision or dream but they do not call it into reality. When I first saw the pear tree, I thought that God was going to give me that many spiritual children through the Bible studies and prayer ministry. I never thought that one day, I would have many churches.

Once a year, all the campuses gathered at the main campus for what we called *"Super Sunday"*. When the churches gathered for *"Super Sunday"* periodically, it was a time when we closed all the other campuses, and gathered at the main campus, which had the largest building.

On one particular *"Super Sunday"*, I recall looking out over the congregation of 1,200 gathered that morning, and I recalled the day God led me to that pear tree. I then understood why God had directed me to that pear tree before I started the churches. God had prophesied to me through that vision ahead of time. When God gives us a vision, we must call it into reality, and put action behind it. That vision became a reality because I called things to be as though they were already, and I obeyed God with my actions.

CHAPTER FIFTEEN

Doing Greater Things

I know some of you reading this book are going to do greater things than I did. I hope this book will inspire you to get started. I never went to school in America, and if I could do this, you can too and more. God has everything but He has one need; to be needed by us. He wants us to trust in Him. I came to realize that trust is faith. If we trust in God, we will respond to His grace, His love, and walk by faith.

Faith is walking in the unknown. Faith means that we trust God for what we are not able to see with our natural eyes. To acquire this kind of faith, we must mature. It takes maturity to walk into the unknown and believe that God's plans are better than ours.

I always saw myself as an extension of the Lord Jesus Christ. I declared this and told the people of the church to also declare this - that we are an extension of the Lord Jesus Christ, to take dominion on Earth, that the glory of God would fill the Earth through us. When we see ourselves as Jesus' body, His hands, and feet, we become what we believe. After all, Jesus said that He is the head, and we are His body. The body is attached to the head. The head guides, and we do it. It's all about Him. We are here to fulfill His purpose. We are His voice. We act on His behalf. We are here to reproduce ourselves and continue the ripple effect.

Our part is to love people, make the weak strong and give them a chance to win in life. Our part is to make serving God enjoyable business. If you are reading this, you are learning the secret to making your investment in God. When you start doing this, you will not experience instant gratification. You sow first, then you reap. In the natural, we invest before we get the return.

1 Timothy 4:15-16 (MSG) says, *"Cultivate these things. Immerse yourself in them. The people will all see you mature right before their eyes! Keep a firm grasp on both your character and your teaching. Don't be diverted. Just keep at it. Both you and those who hear you will experience salvation."*

Run your ministry like Jesus ran His ministry. Jesus trained the twelve. The apostles continued the work and trained others. The apostle Paul would train the people, then the people would go and repeat the same process. A lot of times, people think it is up to the pastor to do everything in ministry, like teach, preach, pray, and go to the hospital. One person cannot do what a hundred people can do. If I would not have had so many dedicated people, I would not have been able to start so many other churches.

Ephesians 4:11-12 (NKJV) says, *"And He Himself gave some to be apostles, some prophets, some evangelists, and some pastors and teachers, for the equipping of the saints for the work of ministry, for the edifying of the body of Christ."*

You see, the pastor feeds and matures the saints. The saints go and do the work of the ministry.

Jesus wants us to help people mature, because as they mature, they multiply. The Holy Spirit has given each Christian a special gift for building up the church.

It is very important to find out what your gift is and look for an opportunity to use your gift. Use your gift to strengthen the church. In doing so, you will find fulfillment for your life. There is no greater satisfaction on Earth than to see other people come to Christ, mature, make more disciples, and then see those disciples do even greater things than you were able to do.

God is asking us to launch into the realm of the impossible; something you can't do on your own. Jesus' desire was that His disciples would do the same works He did and even greater things. My hope is that you will supersede me and do greater things than I did.

CHAPTER SIXTEEN

Graduation

My daughter Tracy attended Oral Roberts University in Tulsa, Oklahoma. After graduation, Tracy met Marcus, a great looking, charming young Christian man who was also Italian. They both fell for each other. He was from Boston, and she was from Michigan. After they met, Tracy came home to Michigan, and Marcus went home to Boston. They started a long-distance relationship. My daughter was not working, so she went to Boston often to get to know him. Marcus could not come to Michigan often because he was helping his parents, who were the pastors of the church. Marcus was very involved in the ministry there.

When Tracy and Marcus got married, they moved to Boston. Tracy worked at the airport while Marcus was doing ministry with his parents. I got along so well with Marcus. I liked his ways – he was charming, charismatic, and personable. I didn't see him as a son-in-law, I saw him as a son.

A year after Tracy and Marcus got married, I had already been teaching and leading Bible studies for nine years. I was functioning like a pastor because I was nurturing and caring for the people. They became my extended family. I was not aware I was a pastor because I thought to be a pastor, you must hear a voice from heaven saying something like, *"I want you to be a pastor."*

My son-in-law, Marcus, made me see that I was a pastor, because of the way I was taking care of people. He came from a fourth generation of ministers, so he knew how to do church. I only knew the Word and how to take care of people. I had no background on how to run a church, but Marcus made me see that as I was teaching and leading the Bible studies, I was already doing what a pastor is supposed to do.

In the Chapter titled *"Starting the Churches"*, I explained how I had gone to Israel and while I was there, a lady had a message for me that God wanted me to start a church. While I was on my return flight home from Israel, I stopped in New York. Tracy met me in New York. Because Tracy was working at the airport, she arranged for me to stay with her in Boston for another week. During my stay in Boston, I told Marcus and Tracy all about what the lady told me about God saying to start my church. I explained that I felt overwhelmed because I did not know how to run a church. This was in September.

That night, Marcus began to ponder in his heart coming to Michigan to help me start our church. He did not say anything to Tracy or me at that time. He was concerned about how he would explain to his parents about his desire to leave their church in Boston and come to Michigan.

At Christmas time of that same year, Marcus and Tracy came to Michigan. A few days before they came, Marcus told Tracy about his desire to help me start a church. He told Tracy that while they were in Michigan for Christmas, he planned to tell me. Tracy did not say anything to me prior to Marcus telling me. While Marcus and Tracy were in Michigan, Marcus said to me, *"Mom, when you told me that God told you to start a church, but you did not know how to do it, a desire came in my heart to come and help you. I have the experience because I saw my grandparents and my parents do church."* That meant that Marcus and Tracy were planning to move from Boston to Michigan.

But there was another concern on my part. Marcus was only 22 years old, and I thought a pastor needed to have more life experience than that. So, I expressed that concern. Marcus said, *"I will attach myself to your hip, and we will do this together. I know how to do church, and you know how to nourish people and we will do this together, I promise you."* I believed him.

On Mother's Day of the next year, we started the church and God did amazing things, as I already talked about. In less than a decade, we already had three churches established and we had many dedicated pastors that took care of the people. Me and my family went to Italy for one month and Marcus was the life of the party. After a week we were in Italy, Marcus started experiencing pain in his throat. We noticed that his throat had swollen, but he was still upbeat because he did not want to spoil the vacation for all of us. That is the kind of person he was.

When we arrived back in the U.S., Tracy and I took Marcus to the doctor. The doctor diagnosed Marcus with lymphoma, and it had already spread to his lymph nodes. The doctor told us that Marcus had only two years to live. When Tracy heard that, she fainted and fell to the floor. Marcus grabbed hold of her and kept saying, *"Tracy, I promise you I will not die."*

For two years, we fought this battle, but Marcus died. Until the last moment, we believed that somehow, Marcus would be healed. The church was devastated over his passing away. We were all devastated. After all, he was only 34 years old, so gifted, so talented and had so much to offer. We buried Marcus. For three days, I could not think straight.

On the third day after Marcus' burial, I was sitting up in my bed around 2:00 PM and I was thinking to myself, *"we have been preaching faith, and Marcus died, and the people are going to think that the message of faith did not work for us, and they are not going to believe us anymore."* I was contemplating closing the church. I thought maybe I could sell the building and pay back some of our big donors because they had believed in our ministry to give above and beyond. I thought we could give the remainder to a good ministry.

Suddenly, Marcus appeared to me at the foot of my bed. He had a full head of hair and looked perfect like he did before he got cancer. Marcus said, *"Why are you thinking those things? Why are you crying? And why are you despairing? I am happy and having so much fun up there. And look at me – I have hair and I am strong!"* as he flexed his arm muscles. *"I love it up there. So, don't think the way you are thinking."* And then, he jokingly spun around like he always used to do when he was well - and then he vanished before my eyes.

When this vision ended, I understood that God gave me two messages. The first message was that Marcus was looking so healthy and hysterically happy. The second message was that God would not be pleased if I closed the church. So, I didn't close the church.

Seeing Marcus fully alive made John 11:26 so real to me; *"And whoever lives and believes in Me shall never die."* It reminded me of when I visited Heaven the first time, that one minute I was on

Earth, and the next minute, I was in Heaven. I concluded then that believers in Jesus do not die. My despair and crying stopped. I still missed him, but I knew that he was fine. As believers, when our time on Earth is over, it is like stepping from one room into another. We graduate from life on this Earth to our eternal life with God.

After dealing with the loss of Marcus, and naturally wondering why he was not healed, I determined that I would not judge the Word according to my experience of Marcus dying. I have witnessed many, many people who have been supernaturally healed. I believe with all my heart that Jesus took the stripes on His body for us to receive healing in this life.

About one year after Marcus' passing, all three Life Christian churches gathered for another *"Super Sunday"*. As I was preparing to give the message for *"Super Sunday"*, I asked God to give me something fresh to tell the people. God amazed me once again.

CHAPTER SEVENTEEN

Second Visit to Heaven

God took me to Heaven for a second time. This is how it began. I was in my kitchen, expecting a message from God for *"Super Sunday"*. It is difficult to explain the supernatural experience, but suddenly, I was taken into a trance, and I heard my doorbell ring. When I went to answer the door, there was an angel standing there. The angel was wearing a long white robe with a blue sash around his waist. Under his arm, he held a rolled-up carpet. The carpet was beige with gorgeous flowers. I was curious to know why he had this carpet under his arm.

The angel took the carpet and rolled it out on the front porch. I noticed the carpet was reflecting the colors of his garment. While I was admiring the carpet, the angel said, *"Get on."* I said, *"That carpet is too beautiful to step on. I don't want to ruin it. I can't get on."* He replied, *"No. Get on!"* Although I was very apprehensive, I stepped on the carpet just to be obedient.

As I stepped on the carpet, the angel put his arm around me and held me. As we stood on the carpet, we started moving. It felt like the carpet was flying us. At first, I was afraid. I thought, *"Oh my!*

What's happening? Where are we going?" But the more we flew, the more I lost my fear because the angel was holding me. Before I knew it, we were in the clouds on this carpet. We ended up in Heaven. The carpet took the angel and me right on the porch of this mansion in heaven. I knew this was my mansion.

As I got off the carpet, I didn't see the angel anymore. I reached for the handle to open the door to the mansion, and it was unlocked. As I stepped inside, a woman was standing there smiling and waiting for me. The woman proceeded to show me every room in the house. I had previously seen the outside of my mansion during my first visit to heaven, which took place almost twenty years before this. This time, I was seeing the inside. The furniture was the same style of furniture I had in my home on Earth, only bigger. As the woman was showing me around, Jesus came, and the woman left.

Jesus and I began strolling together as he continued showing me the house. I saw a vase that looked exactly like a vase I had in my house on Earth, except that it was about three times bigger. As Jesus and I were talking, he pulled ahead, and I hurried to catch up to Him. As I hurried, I accidentally bumped into the vase. It fell off the table, crashed on the ground, and shattered into many pieces. I felt terrible and I didn't even want to look at Jesus because I thought that I had done something wrong by being careless.

Jesus smiled, chuckled, and said, *"Why are you feeling that way?"* I wanted to show Jesus my reverence for Him and replied, *"I didn't mean to do it."* Jesus laughed and said, *"You can't break anything in Heaven! Watch me."* Jesus blew His breath on those pieces. The pieces all came together, and the vase was exactly like before. It looked perfect! There was not even a small crack anywhere. I was amazed.

Jesus and I went outside and started walking. We came to a subdivision. In the subdivision, I saw many different types of houses: ranches, colonials, and larger colonials. All of them were in various stages of construction. Some were completely built. Some had only the foundation laid. Others had only the framework done. Others needed the finishing work.

Then, I was surprised to see a pastor who was serving in one of my churches coming in and out of her home, which was half-built. I said to Jesus, *"She's on Earth serving in my church, but she's in Heaven also."* He chuckled. Then I saw many of the people who were serving with me in my churches on Earth coming in and out of their homes. I said to Jesus, *"These are the people I know on Earth."*

He replied, *"Yes, this is your subdivision that you are building. What you are doing on Earth is getting built over here."* I understood that what my leaders, who were my disciples, were doing in the churches on Earth, was building their houses in heaven and their house was in my subdivision. To my surprise, I saw even a couple of pastors that I trained on Earth, who went to start their own church. They didn't carry the Life Christian Church name, but they were also in my subdivision.

I said to Jesus, *"You mean I'm going to be with all these people I know on Earth and they're going to be with me for all eternity?"* He replied, *"Yes, you're going to live with the people that you know and love on Earth."* For Jesus, it was a matter of fact, but for me, it was a new understanding. I was so happy that I grabbed Jesus' arms with both hands, and I was jumping up and down for joy, saying, *"Oh my God! I'm going to be with them for all eternity."* Jesus looked at me and said, *"I'm in awe of your heart and your love for the people!"* Jesus made me aware of my own heart and the love I had for the people, because I did not realize how much I loved my people.

I do not recall how I returned to Earth from this second visit to Heaven, but when I returned, I was on my front porch. That is when the trance ended, and I found myself in the same spot in my kitchen where I was expecting God to give me a message for *"Super Sunday"*. And, boy, it was quite a message I received from God for both myself and for the people of the church.

On *"Super Sunday"*, I delivered the message to the church. I shared with the congregation my experience of visiting Heaven for a second time, and everyone was encouraged. I emphasized that what the people were doing to help disciple people was already building their houses in Heaven. They all cheered and praised God when I told them that we were together building our own subdivision. The reality that we were going to be together for all eternity was so moving, for we truly loved each other, and we truly understood how much our making of disciples was pleasing God. I felt like a delivery girl giving the reality of Heaven to the people.

CHAPTER EIGHTEEN
How to Achieve Eternal Rewards

What I observed in Heaven and what was repeatedly made real, was that the way people live their lives on Earth determines the rewards they receive in Heaven. As born-again Christians, we will not be judged because God judged sin in Jesus, and we became the righteousness of God in Christ Jesus. Jesus became sin for us, and we took on His righteousness. But we will receive rewards based on how we live our lives on Earth. If we love, respect, and honor people, especially the leaders who imparted truth to us, we will receive great rewards in heaven. This revelation is confirmed throughout the Scriptures. Hebrews 13:7 says, *"Remember your leaders, who spoke the word of God to you. Consider the outcome of their way of life and imitate their faith."* (NIV)

I highly honor the leaders who have imparted the Word of God to me. I have already told you how Bro. Hagin's book, *The Believer's Authority* opened a whole new world to me. I have listened to hundreds of his messages, and many of his other books. I was mentored through his teaching. Even though I did not know him personally, his ministry had a major effect on my life.

And then there is Dr. Paul (David) Yonggi Cho from Korea. The way I was introduced to him was supernatural. I was sleeping soundly and at 3 o'clock in the morning, I heard a voice say, *"Get up – go watch television."* I did not have a television upstairs in my bedroom. So, I went downstairs in the family room, turned on the television, and there was Dr. Paul Yonggi Cho on television at 3 o'clock in the morning. For three months straight I got up at 3 o'clock in the morning to watch him. I was so hungry for the Word.

After those three months, I was talking to a friend mine and told her what I was doing. She said, *"Why are you doing that? You could buy a video recorder and watch it during the day."* I said, *"I did not know that such a thing existed."* She went to buy it and set it up for me. So, I continued to watch his program for years. In every message he gave, Dr. Cho shared a testimony of his own, or those of the people in his church, and it made the message come alive. It made so real to me that God is still working with believers the way He did when Jesus walked on earth. He gave testimonies. The supernatural was not only working for Dr. Cho, but for the people in his church. I learned how to love and help people, but also how to always tell the people the truth. If we don't tell people the truth, nobody learns.

•••

Kenneth Copeland was another teacher I was watching on television. One day, Kenneth's wife Gloria was teaching instead of Kenneth. At that time, I didn't believe in women preaching due to my Catholic and Mormon background. So, when I heard Gloria teaching, I became indignant and was marching toward the television to turn it off. I said to myself out loud, *"Oh, now women too!"* Halfway to the television, I was stopped almost like I could not move. I heard God say, *"What are you doing? I know hearts, I don't know parts!"* Only God could have convinced me that He calls both men and women to teach and preach. I have learned most of what I know through the Holy Spirit who taught me.

I am so ever grateful for these teachers of God that I learned from. When we honor our teachers, it's very pleasing to God. So, what are some of the important ways we build rewards in Heaven? When I was a pastor in Michigan, I had people come to me and say they wanted to be of great assistance to me. They felt called to serve me. I would tell them that I didn't need anything, I have all my needs met. I would say, *"If you want to help me, help the new believers in this church because if you help them, you help me."* Matt 25:40 says, *"The King (God) will reply, 'Truly I tell you, whatever you did for one of the least of these brothers and sisters of mine, you did for me.'"* (NIV)

What's so wonderful about God is that when we receive Jesus into our hearts, He gives us the grace to love others. He deposits His love into us so we can love others with His love. God knows that being selfish creates a lonely life. He wants us to have a rich, fulfilling, and rewarding life on Earth and in Heaven. We obtain that by walking in love.

I had a revelation that God would be pleased with me when I loved and helped baby Christians. I thought, *"what would I do if someone would love and care for my children when they were little?"* I would be so grateful and never forget those who would love my children. So, if we love God, we must also love His children. I always encouraged others to do the same. I have always tried to follow what Jesus said in Matt 7:12 - Therefore, whatever you want men to do to you, do also to them, for this is the Law and the Prophets (NKJV). This is how the leaders in the church, who were my disciples, lived also.

Jesus will reward everyone according to how we treat others. This means truly loving God and His children. You will be enriched in this life, and you can know that God will reward you greatly for all eternity. Revelation 22:12 describes this reward system, *"...Behold, I am coming quickly, and My reward is with Me, to give to everyone according to his work."* (NKJV)

When Jesus said, *"Go therefore and make disciples"* (Matt 28:19), He was not giving a suggestion. He meant for every believer to share the Good News and get busy making disciples, and that is what our ministry is all about. Eternity is for such a long time, it is hard for us to grasp, but eternity in Heaven is far greater than we can ever imagine. I pray that somehow as you've joined me on the journey of my visits to Heaven with Jesus, you have captured a glimpse of what God has in store for you.

CHAPTER NINETEEN

The Testimonies of My Children

I asked my children to write what they remember of our early days as a family. All three of them wrote about how they saw me before and after the day I was saved.

ANTON'S WORDS:

"I remember that morning. I left for school, seeing my mother struggling, depressed, and mopey, as if all the energy she possessed had been drawn out of her for the day. This wasn't the first time I'd seen her this way. This had been happening for a long time. Every day, I thought to myself, *"Mom must be going through a mid-life crisis. Surely this sadness must end soon."* I remember avoiding coming home and spending a lot of time with friends until I 'had' to come home. I just didn't want to see her in this condition; it wasn't a happy time in our home.

However, on this day, and for some reason, I went home right after school, and I was totally surprised with what I saw. Mom was happy, vibrant, and excited! This was such a dramatic change from how I saw her earlier that morning. I was dumbfounded. I really thought she purchased and took drugs to be this excited about life! What I discovered that afternoon was that mom didn't take any drugs but found the one person that took her out of a depressive state – Jesus!

You see, we grew up in a religious household; Jesus was talked about occasionally in the Mormon church, but it was never emphasized to live as Christ lived. As Mom began to live out her born-again experience, I thought to myself, "*how did this happen? This must be a phase of life she is going through. Is this going to end?*" Well, this phase of Mom's life has never ended. If anything, it was the beginning of a better life, for her as well as for our household.

Over a period of time, Mom's demeanor about life with Jesus began to show. Prayers were being answered; communication within our family was getting better; and, most of all, joy was in our home for the first time! This fire my mother had found in Christianity began to affect her, her friends, and anyone she conversed with about Jesus. Mom was determined to tell everyone about the joy she found living for Jesus and it's not surprising that many people have discovered that same joy because of her impact."

DINO'S WORDS:

"I remember coming home from high school every day, deeply concerned for my mother. She grew more depressed each day. I was watching this beautiful mother I loved sinking deeper and deeper into sadness. Being home became difficult. Then, as if someone turned on a switch, she was no longer depressed and sad. In fact, she was happy and full of so much life. I had never seen her like that before—ever. What happened to my mother? At times, it looked like an actual light was shining on her. The change was so dramatic that I first thought she was taking a new drug, but nothing could be further from the truth! She had discovered a very real Jesus who began to do amazing things in her life!

This was so different from our Mormon church experience. This was real. Jesus was real. The atmosphere of our home had completely changed. There was no denying it. So much love was oozing from her that my friends kept making up reasons to come over to be around her! That love was so irresistible that I too found myself receiving Jesus! Miracles, joy, and answered prayers became commonplace in our home. And if that wasn't enough, then my mother had a remarkable visit to Heaven. Yes, Heaven is a real place with a very real Jesus. After that encounter, mom had a greater determination to help others know Jesus and how real Heaven is.

You could always hear her saying, *"Why waste seventy or eighty years living for yourself here on Earth when you can have an eternity to live in Heaven with Jesus!"* My hope is that many more people, after reading her book, will discover the joys of living for Jesus and be convinced that an amazing place called Heaven is waiting for them."

TRACY'S WORDS:

"My mother's story truly reveals the miraculous transformation that God will do to the one who comes fully to Him. My mom was so broken and a complete mess, as most of us are, before she came to Christ. She was so emotionally wrecked and haggard looking. It came to the point that I, along with my brothers, stayed away from the house as much as possible. Our house was just a place to sleep and shelter before starting another day.

One of the main reasons why I welcomed Jesus into my heart was seeing the transformation in her life. The greatest fruit she wore was peace; a peace I desperately wanted. Miracles began to happen in our home as well as much answered prayer. The God in her drove me to surrender my heart to Jesus. It was amazing to watch God's touch on my mom's life and on the ministry God gave her.

One of the most influential times my mom shared with me was when she experienced going to Heaven. It really was a game-changer for me. I realized that Earth was a dress rehearsal for Heaven. I decided to live for Heaven instead of Earth. I truly owe to her all that God is doing in my life."

MY WORDS:

My children shared with you how they saw such a great change in me after I was born again. My friends that I knew for years were inquiring what happened to me. From that time on, I lived for the Kingdom. I told everyone I met that I wanted to affect their lives for the better.

My life has had a ripple effect. It first affected my children; they came to the Lord. Some of my Mormon friends came to the Lord too. The Bible studies I started grew into a church. From one church, we grew to many churches.

As I said before, once a year, we brought all the churches together and we had a *"Super Sunday"*.

I recall one *"Super Sunday"* morning, when the church was full. So many of my spiritual children had gathered that day and my heart was so overjoyed to see them all together. That day, my eyes were opened to see that the pear tree experience had become a reality. I thought, *"Wow, God did what I asked to give me as many spiritual children as the pear tree that was overflowing with pears."* Also, that day, I understood why God changed my name from Marie to Sarah. In the Bible, Abraham and Sarah are seen as the spiritual father and mother of many children. All those people standing in the congregation that day were my many spiritual children. Everyone called me *"Mama,"* even those who were older than me. How incredible is my God to bring what He showed me into reality. The Lord was glorified through my life, and I still want God to be glorified through my life for as long as I live.

CONCLUSION

Do You Want to See Heaven, Too?

Hopefully, this book stirs your desire to want to spend all eternity in heaven with God. This wonderful future is also for you, not just for me. You don't have to wait until you leave this Earth to start enjoying life. You can start right now by receiving Jesus into your heart as your Lord and Savior.

When you connect with Jesus, you connect with the supernatural life. Think about it, God is smarter than the smartest person in the world, and when we receive Jesus, God's Spirit comes and lives inside of us and that Spirit advises and guides us. He helps us see things that we could have never seen in the natural. He helps us accomplish things that in the natural, we would have never accomplished. He helps us understand beyond our natural understanding. Why would anyone settle for less than this? The supernatural life is always better than the natural life and it's available to you.

If you have never invited Him to come into your heart, do it right now. It is very simple. Romans 10:9-10 says: *"That if you confess with your mouth, 'Jesus is Lord,' and believe in your heart that God raised Him from the dead, you will be saved. For it is with your heart that you believe and are justified, and it is with your mouth that you confess and are saved."* (NIV)

Do what the Word says.

I suggest that you kneel down and say:

"Lord, forgive me of my sins. Come into my heart. Be my Savior and be my Lord. Holy Spirit, create a new life in me from this day forward. In Jesus' name. Amen."

You are now born again if you prayed this prayer with a sincere heart. Yes, it is that simple! Congratulations and welcome to the family.

Pastor Sarah Gardner

If you were encouraged by Pastor Sarah's words and would like to hear more of her testimonies or to read more of her books, contact her via the following links:

Email: sarah@sarahgardnerministries.com
Instagram: @sarahgardnerministries
Facebook: @sarahgardnerministries
YouTube: @sarahgardnerministries
Website: www.sarahgardnerministries.com

Mailing Address:
Sarah Gardner Ministries
8374 Market Street #109
Lakewood Ranch, FL 34202

About the Author

 Pastor Sarah Gardner became a born-again Christian through the 700 Club. Years later, the 700 Club produced a program on her dramatic conversion and the ripple effect that her life had on others. Pastor Sarah was ordained by Bishop Keith Butler, the founder and senior pastor of Word of Faith International Christian Center in Southfield, Michigan.

Pastor Sarah planted and pastored seven Life Christian churches in Southeast Michigan. She also founded and pastored Life Christian Church in Naples, Florida. After five years, she left that church to her daughter Tracy Boyd to pastor. It is now known as Grow Church. Sarah Gardner Ministries is focused on ministry online, helping believers mature and know their God in a personal way.

Printed in Great Britain
by Amazon